THE

Negro Mason in Equity:

A PUBLIC ADDRESS

FOR THE PURPOSE OF PLACING BEFORE THE WORLD THE HISTORICAL
FACTS UPON WHICH THE NEGRO MASON IN AMERICA
BASES HIS CLAIM TO LEGITIMACY AND
CONSEQUENT RIGHTS,

— BY —

M∴ W∴ SAMUEL W. CLARK,

Grand Master of Colored Masons of the State of Ohio.

ISBN: 978-1-63923-833-0

Printed: March 2023

Published and Distributed By:
Lushena Books
607 Country Club Drive, Unit E
Bensenville, IL 60106
www.lushenabks.com

ISBN: 978-1-63923-833-0

INTRODUCTION.

At the Thirty-fourth Annual Communication of the Grand Lodge of Free and Accepted Masons for the State of Ohio and Jurisdiction, held in Cleveland, Ohio, August 12, 1884, I, as Grand Master, in my official address submitted the following for the consideration of the Craft:

"With our centennial year come greater duties and consequent responsibilities. The time is full at hand when we must no longer depend upon our friends to do battle for us. The fight must be our own. Neither must it be a defensive one; we must be aggressive; we must assert ourselves; we must tear away the flimsy mask behind which the white American Mason takes refuge from the penetrating eye of Truth and Justice. Let us turn upon him the fierce light of recorded history, thereby disclosing to the open gaze of the world the false, unjust, and un-Masonic position which he assumes. To this end I would recommend the preparation of an address, to be submitted to the world at large, of such scope as to meet all points at issue."

The Committee on Grand Master's Address, to whom my address was referred, reported as follows:

"*Resolved*, That the recommendation to appoint a committee to issue an address to the world at large—in relation to the position and legality of colored Masons—be approved, and that M∴ W∴ Grand Master Samuel W. Clark shall be chairman of said committee."

This report was unanimously adopted, and by virtue of the authority conferred therein this address has been prepared; and in accordance with a resolution adopted at the Thirty-fifth Annual Communication of the Grand Lodge, the same is now published and distributed gratuitously.

The negro Mason has never been recognized by the white American Masons, officially, as a just and legal Mason, although many, having from a careful examination of history satisfied themselves of his genuineness and authenticity, have done so unofficially. He has been termed spurious, clandestine, irregular, and every thing else but a true and regular Mason. Two reasons may be given as the chief ones for this unjust position taken by the white Masons of the United States: First, the general ignorance of the great mass of American Masons concerning our origin and history; secondly, the bitter prejudice which so many white Americans have against the negro. This prejudice, which seems to be almost inherent, if not wholly so, renders them unfit to do justice to the negro Mason; they either refuse to examine the records of history for fear they may discover that the negro's right is equal to theirs, or, knowing the facts, they endeavor to subvert them by misstatements and false reasoning. Thus, the large mass of white American Masons having no information of their own, but depending wholly upon the *ex parte* statements of prejudiced minds, formulate their opinions accordingly, and readily unite in the almost universal cry of illegitimacy and irregularity.

We are inclined to believe that the great body of the Craft, notwithstanding the bitter prejudices against us, will deal justly with our cause when once they are clearly informed concerning it; we can not yet believe that the great body of the Craft will be false to the doctrines and tenets of their profession; we believe that Truth, Justice, and Brotherly Love must prevail.

Therefore we submit this address, first, to the Fraternity at large, so that it may be fully advised concerning our history, and have no excuse for failing to right a wrong that has existed for more than a century; secondly, we submit it to the world at large, so that it may know upon what grounds we base our claims to legitimacy and consequent rights. And if these rights be granted us, new honors will be won by our Ancient and Honorable Institution, and its members clothed with a higher sense of justice will receive commendations of praise from their fellow-men; but if they are denied us, we will appeal to the world at large, where, at the bar of public opinion, we will submit our cause, feeling confident of a just verdict, which will be manifested by the marking of all those who refuse us as a multitude of hypocrites professing all the virtues but acting as veritable shams, and belying the sublime principles of an institution which has for its chief corner-store the "Brotherhood of man because of the Fatherhood of God."

The chief aim in preparing this address has been, first, to state in simple and plain language the exact facts concerning the origin and growth of Masonry among colored men in America; secondly, to refute the false reasonings of our enemies; and thirdly, to make a comparison between the history of the white Mason and the negro Mason of America.

We have chosen the title "Negro Mason" in preference to "Colored Mason," first, because the term "colored" can be as correctly applied to the Mongolian, the Malay, the Indian, or the Australian, as to the African, or the American of African descent, and we desire the title to indicate with certainty the party at bar; secondly, we are loyal to our African blood. Whatever of wrong we have suffered has been because of our African descent; and now if the right is to be done to us, we want it because it is ours to have; and we want it given to us not under the softening appellation of "colored American," but as wearing the badge of the African negro, having with all humanity a common Fatherhood in God.

The greatest care has been taken to state nothing as a historical fact but what can be authenticated by records now in existence and accessible to all students of Masonic history. Nothing has been guessed at, nothing has been surmised. We therefore present you an address, not made up with fanciful pictures drawn from the imagination, but a plain, substantial statement of facts.

Our acknowledgments are due to Ill. ∴ Bro. Enoch T. Carson and R∴. W∴. Bro. John D. Caldwell, editor of *New Day and New Duty*, for their kindness in allowing us free access to their Masonic libraries, by which means we were enabled to verify all the facts stated herein; also are we indebted to the Reports on Foreign Correspondence made by M∴. W∴. Bro. Wm. T. Boyd to our own Grand Lodge. To all these brethren we return our thanks.

We ask that you may give what here follows your most careful attention and consideration, with the hope that whatever prejudices you may have against us will be dispelled, and having your minds illuminated by the facts of history, you will be impelled thereby to lift up your voices in the defence of Truth and Justice, and "Render unto Cæsar the things which are Cæsar's."   S. W. C.

THE NEGRO MASON IN EQUITY,

—BY—

M∴ W∴ Bro. Samuel W. Clark.

Underlying every institution, whether human or divine, there are certain cardinal principles, tenets, and doctrines. And according to their merit as impressed upon the mind of man these institutions have grown and flourished, or have dwindled and decayed. Consequently, those that have become most extensive in their domain, and have withstood longest against the lapse of time, the scrutiny of reason, and the venom of prejudice, are entitled to the highest degree of merit.

Occupying a high place among these meritorious institutions, accepting the above measurement as true, is the most ancient and Honorable Fraternity of Free and Accepted Masons.

With becoming pride the enthusiastic Mason discourses in eloquent language upon the antiquity and universality of Masonry, and upon the sublimity of its principles. Upon the airy wings of imagination he will transport you to the Garden of Eden or to the tower of Babel; by the aid of tradition he will take you to the building of Solomon's Temple, 1000 B. C.; or, if you be not satisfied with this, by the aid of documentary and historical evidence he will carry you to the foundation of the Colleges of Builders, instituted by Numa Pompilius, 715. B. C. All this will he do to prove its antiquity. To prove its universality he will tell you that among the devotees around its altars may be found the fair-skinned Caucasian and the dark-hued African, the almond-eyed Mongolian and the copper-colored Indian. He will tell you that neither race nor creed nor clime nor condition is a barrier to an entrance into its sanctuaries.

But this generalization is not satisfactory. Permit me to present to you the authorized expressions of leading Masonic scholars and eminent American Masons upon some of the principles and tenets of our institution, and which have been adopted as the line of action for all

Masons. Many of these quotations we have found in Bro. John D. Caldwell's *New Day-New Duty*. We select, first, from the *Craftsman*, the text relating to that chief tenet, BROTHERLY LOVE:

"By the exercise of brotherly love we are taught to regard the whole human species as one family—the high and low, the rich and poor—who, as created by one Almighty Parent, and inhabitants of the same planet, are to aid, support, and protect each other. On this principle, Masonry unites men of every country, sect, and opinion, and conciliates true friendship among those who might otherwise have remained at a perpetual distance."

The following passages relating to this tenet are quoted from "Illustrations of the Symbols of Masonry," by Jacob Ernst (p. 200):

"Upon the merits of this virtue we place our institution second to none. Its influence will accomplish what others fail to do. It is a bond of union that draws man to his fellow-man, however widely apart; gives mutual confidence and protection, whatever his caste or creed may be—a brother TRUE will ever recognize a brother's hail.

"The potency of this principle exists in the fact that Masonry unequivocally excludes from its halls every thing that is at variance with the requirements of a universal brotherhood."

On this same topic Gadicke says:

"He who does not find his heart warmed with love toward all mankind should never strive to be made a Freemason, for he can not exercise brotherly love."

At the great Masonic banquet in St. Louis, September, 1868, Bro. Albert Pike said:

"God pity the man who will not lay on the altar of Masonry every feeling of ambition, every feeling of ill-will in his heart toward a brother Mason, no matter what rite you may believe, at what altar of Masonry you may worship. Freemasonry is one faith, one great religion, one great common altar, around which all men, of all tongues and all languages can assemble; in which there can be no rivalry, except a noble emulation of rites, orders, and degrees, which can best work and best agree.

"And Masonry will never be true to her mission till we all join hands, heart to heart, and hand to hand, around the altar of Masonry with a determination that Masonry shall become at some time worthy of her pretensions—no longer a pretender to that which is good; but that she shall be *an apostle of peace, good-will, charity, and* TOLERATION."

Grand Master Griswold, of the Grand Lodge of Minnesota, in his address to the Grand Lodge, says:

"Masonry knows no sects, no religions, as such; no castes, no nationalities; no black, no white. The color line is not found in Masonry; it has no place there. It is at war with all its teachings. To introduce it would be to mar the symmetry of our beautiful temple, and to give the lie to our words when we say that we believe in the Brotherhood of man because of the Fatherhood of God."

Grand Master Farnell, of the Grand Lodge of New South Wales, in his address when installed as Grand Master, says:

"Political connections and attachments is one thing, and Masonic another thing. The former has its geographical bounds or limits, and is confined to nations or countries; the latter has no bounds or limits, it embraces all nations, and is so universal that it admits of no exclusion amidst the worthy portion of God's creatures; climate, country, color, education, or religion, make no difference. Let this universal bond of union be broken by political geographical boundaries, by the difference of nationalities and peoples, and we become a rope of sand and lose that strength, weight, and influence which concord and unanimity will secure to us."

Grand Master A. H. Battin, of Ohio, in his address to the Grand Lodge in 1875, says:

"But whether he comes from the jungles of Africa, the swamps of Carolina, the plains of Hindoostan, the sands of Arabia, the snow-capped summits of Norway, the Emerald Isle, the sunny fields of France, or from whatever nation or clime he may have traveled, if *he is a Mason*, and can prove himself such, he should be welcomed as a man and a brother into our Lodges and entitled to equal rights in our great brotherhood. The boast of Masons has been that its votaries possess the same mystic language in every clime, that its language is universal, entitled to recognition wherever heard or manifested, and that all Masons, in the character of Masons, stand upon the most perfect equality."

Grand Master Whitehead, of New Jersey, in his address to the Grand Lodge in 1868, says:

"The central idea of Masonry—the foundation stone upon which the superstructure rests—is the recognition and practical application of the great principle of the universal brotherhood of man, whether he drew his first breath amid polar snows or under the burning sun of the tropics; whether he owe political allegiance to an empire, a kingdom, or a republic; whether he be clothed in the purple of Dives or the rags of Lazarus; whether his skin be bleached with the hue of Caucasian, or be clouded with the 'shadow'd livery of the burnish'd sun;' whether he worships his God in a Methodist Meeting-house, an Episcopal Church, a Catholic Cathedral, a Jewish Synagogue, or a Mohammedan

Mosque. The great lesson which Masonry teaches to its votaries is, that

'A man is a man for a' that.'

"The great heart of humanity, weary of the unceasing and harassing strife of this busy and selfish world, where

'The natural bond
Of brotherhood is severed as the flax
That falls asunder at the touch of fire,'

longs for some common platform where contentions can never reach it more. And this eager longing of the human heart the Masonic institution alone can satisfy. Here we are all citizens of one country, which is the great globe itself; members of one family, which is the entire human race; children of one Father, which is God. And this I conceive is the true idea of the institution of Masonry."

Grand Master Gardner, of Massachusetts, in his address to the Grand Lodge, 1870, says:

"The institution of Freemasonry is universal. It stretches from East to West, from North to South, and embraces within itself the representatives of every branch of the human family. Its carefully tiled doors swing open, not at the knock of every man, but at the demand of every true and worthy man duly accepted, whatever his religion, his race, or his country may be.

"This Grand Lodge stands upon the high vantage ground of this catholic society, and recognizes the great principles which must necessarily underlie an institution which has a home on the continents and on the islands of the sea.

"We bear upon the Mason's arms of Massachusetts, and have inscribed upon our Grand Lodge banner, 'Man every where our brother.'"

In an address made by Bro. Robert Hall, of Massachusetts, we find the following:

"The wisdom of Masonry is exemplified in establishing her basis on the immutable foundations of truth. The shackles fell from the hands of prejudice and bigotry at the entrance of her shrine. . . . In her sacred retreat every discordant voice is hushed, and the bitterness of sectarian strife is abashed into silence in the awful presence of pure and absolute Truth. On any platform than this she could not comprehend in her embrace all the tribes of men, as the human race now exists, or has ever existed. It is the recognition of these principles, and the acknowledgment of corresponding obligations, which alone render it possible to make her privileges available to the whole of the great human family. If she should require any other creed than that God is our Father, and that men are his children, and therefore bound to love him and one another, her grand object would at

once be defeated. . . . Next to allegiance to God, and spring-
ing from it its controlling principle, is love for man as man. . . .
Masonry meets man in all the varieties of his condition with sym-
pathy, and comprehends him in all the wants of his complex nature.
She esteems every man the peer of his fellow in nature and rights.
Before her altar distinctions vanish, and all men meet on the level.
The prince and the peasant stand alike in her presence. Whatever is
common to man is not foreign to her regard.''

From an address made to the Grand Lodge of Iowa, Bro. Wm. R.
Whitaker, of Louisiana, chairman of the Committee on Foreign Com-
munications, in reviewing Iowa, selects the following, and gives it his
indorsement as exhibiting a true Masonic spirit:

"The great central idea of Masonry is the doctrine of a universal
brotherhood, with 'charity to all.' Notwithstanding its antiquity and
the illustrious names found among its patrons in all ages and countries,
if it have not charity it is nothing; not the charity of the Priest and
Levite that, standing in the immediate presence of human suffering,
asks 'Who is my neighbor?' but the charity of the Good Samaritan,
which in its comprehensive compassion regards every man as a brother,
of whatsoever nation or kindred or tongue or people. It stops not to
ask whether the sufferer follows Calvin, Wesley, or Fox, nor whether
he is Christian, Jew, or Turk; a charity that knows no difference between the cross of Christ and the crescent of Mohammed, but lovingly
regards every one as a child of the 'Great Father,' 'who heeds and
holds them all in his large love and boundless thought.' "

Thus might we fill page after page with beautiful quotations enliv-
ened, like the foregoing, with the true spirit of Masonry, for its literature abounds in such lofty and sublime expressions of sentiment as
have here been given you. We feel, however, that these are sufficient to indicate the prevailing sentiment of the eminent Masons of
the North and the South, the East and the West. And after all, is it
nothing but sentiment? Is there nothing practical in all these utterances? Are they so many empty, meaningless words spoken only to
catch the plaudits of unthinking listeners? or are they meant to have
application only to the races other than the negro? It would seem so;
for, in America, more than twenty thousand negro Masons, free and
accepted, true and worthy, stand knocking at the "carefully tiled
doors" of the white American Mason, but they "swing not open to
their knock." Here in America there stand to-day more than twenty
thousand negro Masons demanding of the white American Mason that
he prove by his works the realism of the beautiful sentiment "Man is
every-where our brother." But he answers not to the demand. With

perfect rhetoric and eloquent language he will proclaim that "Masonry is established on the immutable foundation of truth," and has for its central idea the "doctrine of a universal brotherhood." But we say to him your professions are not sustained by works, and that you do "give the lie to your words when you say you believe in the 'Brotherhood of man because of the Fatherhood of God.'"

But we would not say that all are so; for, engraven on the tablets of our memories, in letters of shining gold, are the names of true and noble-hearted men who, imbued with the true principles of Masonry, have, not in canting words, but in practical reality, "joined heart to heart and hand to hand around the altar of Masonry with a determination that Masonry shall become at some time worthy of her pretensions—no longer a *pretender* of that which is good, but that she shall be an APOSTLE OF PEACE, GOOD-WILL, CHARITY, and TOLERATION." From across old briny ocean there comes to us, wafted by the winds of "Equality, Liberty, and Fraternity," the names of Morgenstern and Glitza, Barthelmes and Findel, Thevenot and Caubet, Kemeny and Beigel, Castellazzo and Braband, Santiago and Wholey, Marbach and Grimaux, Scaria and Weisman, and a host of others; from the "land of the free and the home of the brave," Minnesota sends a Griswold; Iowa, a Peck; Illinois, a Robbins; Massachusetts, a Norton; and Ohio, our own "Buckeye State," in solid phalanx, a Bierce, a Carson, a Wilmer, a Woodward, a Werner, and a Pike, with Asa H. Battin at its head and John D. Caldwell, with "*New Day, New Duty*," as its support.

These and the many others associated with them in the battle for the supremacy of the right shall surely have their reward.

On the other hand are the myriads who would crush us if they could—men whom we meet in the daily mart, before whose tribunals we plead for justice, and to whose holy teachings we reverently bow. And you ask, is it possible that these upright and honorable men can be so unjust as to deny you that which justly belongs to you? Alas, too true, they do! But they are well skilled in logic, and, if you but listen without investigating, they will prove to you that we are but cheats and impostors, and consequently their actions just and proper. Therefore, we ask you to come with us, and, with the lamp of history, examine their reasons for our rejection and see whether they be not sophisms. If ye be fair-minded men, we fear not the result. "Truth is mighty and will prevail."

So far as we have been able to ascertain, the following are all the reasons that are urged against our recognition as Free and Accepted Masons:

1. That there is a doubt as to whether Prince Hall and his associ-ates were ever made Masons.

2. That if they were made Masons, it was in an Army Lodge without proper authority.

3. That if they were legally made Masons they had no right to exist as an organized body, as is claimed they did from 1775 to 1787, when a warrant, as claimed, was received from the Grand Lodge of England.

4. That no warrant was ever received from England. That what purported to be a warrant was a forged, falsified document.

5. That if received, it was returned to England for correction but never again received in America, a mutilated copy being used in its stead.

6. That if a warrant was granted them it was a violation of the territorial rights of the "Massachusetts Grand Lodge."

7. That if they were legally warranted it was only as a subordinate Lodge; and that it was an assumption of authority on the part of Prince Hall to establish lodges in Philadelphia, and Providence, R. I.; and, that the Grand Lodge established in Boston, in 1808, with African Lodge, No. 459, and the Lodges in Philadelphia and Providence was an irregular body, and as a consequence all its descent is illegal and clandestine.

8. That after the death of Prince Hall, in 1807, the Lodge became dormant, and had thereafter no actual existence.

9. That in 1813, upon the union of the Grand Lodges of England, African Lodge, which had been registered as No. 459, and subsequently as 370, was removed from the list and was never after recognized by the United Grand Lodge of England.

10. That by the Declaration of Independence made by the African Lodge in June, 1827, its existence, if it had any, came to an end.

11. That by the surrender of its warrant to the National Grand Lodge in 1847, it lost its character as a Grand Lodge.

12. That we were not free-born, and therefore could not be made Masons.

13. That our Lodges and Grand Lodges violate the "American Doctrine of Exclusive Territorial Jurisdiction, and therefore have no legal right to exist."

We now propose to take up these objections in the order enumerated, and shall endeavor to prove that they have no basis for their support.

1. That there is a doubt as to whether Prince Hall and his associates were ever made Masons.

The history of their initiation is as follows:

In the early part of 1775, when Boston was garrisoned by British troops, the Masons connected with General Gage's command held lodge meetings at headquarters. Prince Hall, the leading free colored citizen of Boston, was invited to initiation. He considered the matter and made up his mind to join. One night, shortly after, he went alone to the headquarters of General Gage, was admitted to Masonry and raised to the sublime degree of a Master Mason. This made him the first of African descent initiated into the order in the United States, or Colonies at that time. Other free colored citizens of Boston were invited to join the Masons, and on March 6, 1775, Cyrus Jonbus, Buesten Slinger, Thomas Sanderson, Prince Tayden, Cato Speain, Boston Smith, Peter Best, Fortin Howard, Prince Rees, John Canten, Peter Freeman, Benjamin Tiber, Duff Buform, and Richard Tilley were initiated at Castle William, Boston Harbor, now Fort Independence, by Master Batt.

Each of the above candidates paid for entering, fifteen guineas; for passing, seven guineas; for raising, three guineas.

To these brethren there was revealed, on that memorable day, those secrets which Masonic tradition informs us may be traced to the building of the Temple, and the essential principle of which has its germ in the creation of life.

The motive of the English Masons in initiating the first fifteen colored men into the fraternity in this country has been and is still questioned. It is claimed by many that it was done in order to secure the co-operation of the negroes in this country with the British. If this was their motive, they failed in securing its end, for Prince Hall, one of the original fifteen, appears upon the Revolutionary rolls of the State of Massuchussetts as one of the earliest enlisted men in the service of the country against the British. Again it is claimed that these English Masons were influenced by entirely different motives. Recognizing the principle, "By the exercise of brotherly love we are taught to regard the whole human species as one family,"t which was adopted by the Grand Lodge of England, in 1717, i followed as a natural conclusion that these fifteen colored men were made Masons in order that this principle might be proved in recogniz-

ing a race which was the most degraded and brutally treated of the
world.   To this latter view colored Masons, generally, give their
assent.

The records of the initiation of these fifteen colored men is in
possession of the Prince Hall Grand Lodge of Massachusetts.

Following is the testimony of learned Masons and historical students upon this same point:

M. W. Grand Master Gardner, of Massachusetts, in his address to
the Grand Lodge in 1870, says:

"I have *no doubt* that, on the 6th of March, 1775, the day after
Warren delivered his celebrated oration in the Old South Church,
where he was menaced by British troops, Prince Hall and thirteen
others received the three degrees in a traveling lodge attached to one
of the British regiments in the army of General Gage, by whom Boston was then garrisoned."

The record of the initiation supplemented with the testimony of
such an eminent Mason and scholar as William Sewall Gardner, who,
probably, has given more study and research to this particular question
than any other white Mason in America, should be sufficient to
establish the falsity of the first objection, and to remove all doubts
concerning our origin; and especially so when it is remembered that
his historical researches are not for our benefit, but for our destruction.
He is entitled to the credit, however, of being a true historian, although his conclusions are not always philosophical.

We desire, however, to introduce a few more witnesses.

At the annual session of the Grand Lodge of white Masons of the
State of Ohio, held in Cleveland, Ohio, 1875, Grand Master Asa H.
Battin, in his address, gave considerable attention to colored Masonry.
This part of his address was referred to a special committee composed
of the following eminent Masons: Lucius V. Bierce, Past Grand
Master; Enoch· T. Carson, Past Master; Ferdinand Wilmer, Past
Master; Louis H. Pike, Past Master; Charles A. Woodward, Grand
Master, 1876.   Among the conclusions which they reported are the
following:

"Your committee deem it sufficient to say that *they* are satisfied
beyond all question that colored Freemasonry had a legitimate beginning in this country as much so as any other Freemasonry; in fact it
came from *the same source.*

"Your committee have the most satisfactory and conclusive evidence that these colored Freemasons practice the very same rites and
ceremonies, and have substantially the same esoteric or secret modes

of recognition as are practiced by ourselves and by the universal family of Freemasons throughout the world."

We think this is ample testimony in relation to the first objection; and even if we had no testimony but the subsequent fact that they were granted a warrant by the Grand Lodge of England, this, to fair minded men, would be proof conclusive that they were indeed Free and Accepted Masons. It is not to be presumed that the Grand Lodge of England would grant a warrant to a body of men unless she were fully satisfied that they were just and legal Masons.

We now pass to the second objection:

2. That if they were made Masons, it was in an Army Lodge without proper authority.

It is already established that they were made Masons in an Army Lodge. Now let us see if an Army Lodge was an unauthorized, unusual, or illegal body of Masons. If not, then the second objection falls.

W. ∴ Bro. ∴ Henry J. Parker, in an address on "Army Lodges," read before the Worshipful Master's Association in the Masonic Temple, Boston, March 7, 1884, makes the following statements:

"Regimental Lodges appear to have been warranted in the British Army early in the last century, and have undoubtedly exerted a large influence in spreading the tenets of Freemasonry in all parts of the civilized globe.

"The earliest warrant issued for forming an Army Lodge in this country was issued by the St. John's Grand Lodge in 1756, when 'the R. W. Master authorized by his charter of deputation the R. W. Richard Gridley, Esq., to congregate all Free and Accepted Masons in the present expedition against Crown Point, and form them into one or more lodges as he should think fit, and to appoint wardens and other officers to a Lodge pertaining.'

"In 1758 a warrant or dispensation was granted to the 'R. W. Edward Huntingford to hold a Lodge in his Majesty's Twenty-eighth Regiment stationed at Louisburg.' "

In following W. Bro. Parker, we find that quite a number of Lodges were formed by the Provincial Grand Master. It therefore was not an unusual thing for them to exist. Further along we find the following:

"With the arrival of the British troops in Boston Harbor, just before the breaking out of the Revolutionary war, came several Regimental Lodges; for a time their presence was welcomed by the Lodges of the town, but in the controversy which soon began to rage between the Ancients and Moderns their presence only added fuel to the flames."

Evidently in one of these Lodges, not formed by the Provincial Grand Masters, but having original authority from the Mother Grand Lodge in England, was Prince Hall and his associates entered, passed, and raised.

From this same authority and others equally reliable, we learn that on the 15th day of February, 1776, a dispensation was granted to Joel Clark, Esq., to establish an Army Lodge, appointing him and constituting him Master of the American Union Lodge. Would time and space permit, it would be interesting to trace this Lodge through its vicissitudes and periods of dormancy until it became a constituent part of the Grand Lodge of Ohio (white). We may have occasion to refer to this Lodge again. What we wish to say now is, that if an Army Lodge was good enough, and legal enough, and regular enough, with only a dispensation from a Deputy Provincial Grand Master, to form a constituent part of the white Grand Lodge of the State of Ohio, then, in our opinion, a warranted Army Lodge under the authority of the Grand Lodge of England was good enough, and legal enough, and regular enough, to make Prince Hall and his fourteen associates free and accepted Masons.

We are told, however, that we have not yet touched the point; that the lack of authority lies in this. That in 1773 the Massachusetts Grand Lodge placed this limitation upon all Army Lodges :

"That an Army Lodge should not make a Mason of a Civilian, without express authority and permission from the Grand Lodge within whose territory it was commorant at the time."

At this time, 1773, there were two Provincial Grand Lodges exercising concurrent authority in the colony of Massachusetts, the "American doctrine of Grand Lodge jurisdiction" not yet having been introduced. One of these Grand Lodges was the St. John's Grand Lodge, a Provincial Grand Lodge under English authority, with R. W. John Rowe, Esq., Grand Master of North America, at its head. The other of these Grand Lodges was the St. Andrew's, or Massachusetts Grand Lodge, a Provincial Grand Lodge under Scotland, with M. W. Joseph Warren, Esq., Grand Master of the continent of North America, at its head. It was this Grand Lodge that adopted the "limitation" regulation. At this same time there were aslo several Army Lodges located in the colony of Massachusetts, some of which held authority from the Grand Lodge of Ireland, some from the Grand Lodge of Scotland, and others from the Grand Lodge of England.

The point we desire to make is, that each Grand Lodge exercised authority over only the Lodges of its constituency, and, therefore, the " limitation ". enacted by the St. Andrew's, or Massachusetts Grand Lodge, could only have force with its own Lodges. If either of the Grand Lodges in Massachusetts could have placed a limitation upon the Army Lodge, in which Prince Hall and his associates were made Masons, which was a regularly warranted Lodge under the direct jurisdiction of the Grand Lodge of England, it would have been St. John's Grand Lodge, which was a Provincial Grand Lodge under English authority.

But we contend that neither of these Provincial Grand Lodges had any jurisdiction over this Army Lodge, and, therefore, had no right to make any limitation as to its reception of candidates. At this time, 1773, the " American doctrine of exclusive territorial jurisdiction" not having been thought of, the several Grand Lodges exercising authority in Massachusetts did so concurrently. This view is agreed in by Bro. Chas. Moore, Past Grand Secretary of the Grand Lodge of Massachusetts, and also editor of the *Free Mason's Monthly Magazine.* In his " Memorial Address" to the St. Andrew's Lodge, December 23, 1869, he says, in defending the establishment of St. Andrew's Lodge, " Massachusetts, like all the other colonies and dependencies of the British Crown, was open and free to the joint occupancy of the three Grand Lodges of that kingdom; namely, England, Scotland, and Ireland." And, as stated in Mackey's Jurisprudence, page 422, " The jurisdiction exercised in this condition of Masonry by the different Grand Lodges *is not over the territory*, but over the Lodge or Lodges which each of them has established." Again, according to Mackey's Jurisprudence, page 313, " A warrant having been granted by the Grand Lodge, the body of Masons thus constituted form at once a constituent part of the Grand Lodge. They acquire permanent rights which can not be violated by any assumption of authority, nor abrogated except in due course of Masonic law." Now this Army Lodge, not having been warranted by the St. Andrew's Grand Lodge, did not form a constituent part thereof, and was, therefore, not under its jurisdiction; consequently, it was an " assumption of authority" on the part of the St. Andrew's Grand Lodge to interfere with the right of this Army Lodge holding a charter from the Grand Lodge of England. Among these " permanent rights" of a warranted Lodge are, " *The right to do all the work of ancient craft Masonry*," and " *The right to increase its members by the admission of new members*," provid-

ing the ancient regulations of the order be not violated.   This Army
Lodge, in making Prince Hall and his associates Masons, did what it
had the right to do, and in doing so violated none of the ancient
regulations of the order, and for what it did, it was responsible to the
Grand Lodge of England only.

The adoption of this resolution of "limitation" in 1773, by the St.
Andrew's Grand Lodge, was the result of the controversy then existing between the "Moderns" and the "Ancients."   There were no
negro Masons then.   But in the labored effort to prove that we are
irregular, this "limitation" resolution has been brought forward to do
a duty entirely foreign to its original purpose.   To such desperation
have our enemies come.   If they would be fair in the application of
this restriction we would not complain.   But they are not.   The records of American Union Lodge, an Army Lodge instituted by the St.
John's Grand Lodge, will show that a number of civilians were made
Masons therein without permission from any one.   And this same
American Union Lodge is now one of the constituent Lodges of the
Grand Lodge of Ohio (white), but no one has ever raised a question
concerning the regularity of the civilians made Masons therein.   Why
the difference?   Because Prince Hall and his associates were black
men.   However, let the argument be what it may, the Grand Lodge
of England by subsequently granting a charter to Prince Hall and his
fourteen associates, made Masons at Castle William March 6, 1775,
decided the question for all time that they were just and legal and
regular Masons, and that it possessed ample authority for its acts in
so doing.   We are willing to abide by her judgment.

3.   That if they were legally made Masons, they had no right to
exist as an organized body, as is claimed they did from 1775 to 1787,
when a warrant, as is claimed, was received from the Grand Lodge of
England.

Whether Prince Hall and his associates had any documentary authority empowering them to meet as a Lodge of Masons from 1775 to
1787, we are not fully prepared to say.   We have seen it stated that
they had a dispensation, and although this is not sustained by any
direct proof, yet we are of the opinion that Prince Hall had some
form of written authority.

Bro. William Sewall Gardner, of Massachusetts, in his address in
1870, in commenting on this point in order to prove that no dispensation was held by these brethren, says:

"Dispensations for Lodges, as preliminary to granting a charter, were not made use of in those days. But more than all there was no authorized power here to grant such dispensation save Provincial Grand Masters Rowe and Warren. A traveling lodge, although attached to a British regiment, could not authorize these persons to assemble as a Lodge. This claim," that a dispensation existed, "is nowhere stated directly, and contains so little foundation that it is not worth considering."

Well, let us consider Bro. Gardner's statement. If, as Bro. Gardner states, "dispensations were not made use of in those days, as preliminary to granting charters," then Prince Hall and his associates needed none. They had the same right to assemble as a Lodge until they received their charter, as any body of white Masons had. Now then, if we can find any body of white Masons that assembled as a Lodge without any documentary authority to do so, and which has subsequently been received and acknowledged as a just and legal Lodge of Masons, then must all objection to African Lodge, No. 459, on these grounds fall. We think we know of one such body. Give us your attention. We will cite two instances which will show a similar condition of circumstances as is said to have existed in the case of Prince Hall and his associates. First, we will call Saint John's Lodge, Boston, said to have been founded July 30, 1733, by Henry Price, Provincial Grand Master of Massachusetts. Concerning this Lodge, Bro. Joseph Robbins, of Illinois, in his review of Massachusetts in 1871, says:

"St. John's Lodge, organized in 1733, was an unauthorized and irregular body until legalized in 1737, when Tomlinson received his deputation from the Grand Master of England."

Bro. James William Hughan, Masonic Historiographer, of England, confirms this when he says, "Boston Lodge is the first that we can find mentioned in any list of Lodges under the Grand Lodge of England, and that in the *list of 1738*." [For Com. Grand Lodge of Ohio (white), 1874, p. 15.]

The original deputation by which authority it is claimed the first Lodge of white Masons was constituted can not be found, and it is not known, so far as records show, that Henry Price was deputized a Provincial Grand Master in 1733. In fact, he is stigmatized by Bro. Norton, of Massachusetts, who is known as a careful historical investigator, as a "swindler and impostor." This is sustained by the following correspondence:

2

"In 1768, November 29th, Thomas French, Grand Secretary at London, wrote to Henry Price, 'I can't account for it why in the list of Provincial Grand Masters the name of Price does not appear.' He chides him for his lack of correspondence, and says, 'that the *earliest record on his book for that part of America is* 1736, *of the deputation of Robert Tomlinson.'"—[New Day, New Duty,* p 35, from G. Sec. Dove.]

From Bro. John Dove's history of the Grand Lodge of Virginia, page 61, we find the following relation to the introduction of Masonry in Massachusetts:

"They commenced their organization by the interposition of Provincial Grand Masters, and at once and immediately by patent [not to be found] from the Grand Lodge of England, granted to R. W. Henry Price, in 1733, opened a Lodge at Boston called the St. John's Grand Lodge, on the 30th of July; *though their* FIRST *regularly installed and* INVESTED *Grand Master* was R. W. Robert Tomlinson, in April, 1737."

This seems sufficient to prove that Henry Price acted without any authority.

From the Grand Lodge proceedings of Massachusetts, 1870, p. 429, we extract the following:

"St. John's Lodge, Boston—This was the first Lodge in Boston; established by Henry Price, Provincial Grand Master, July 30th, 1733. No. written charter was given until one was granted by Provincial Grand Master Rowe."

Now Rowe was not appointed Provincial Grand Master until 1768. Even admitting that the acts of Henry Price were legal and with proper authority, which, we believe, we have proven were not, the fact remains that from 1733 to 1768—a period of thirty-five years— St. John's Lodge, of Boston, existed without a warrant. Now, if St. John's Lodge could exist from 1733 to 1738 without any legal authority, and from 1738 to at least 1768, if not further, without a charter, then may not African Lodge with equal grace and legality have existed from 1775 to 1787 without a charter? and especially so, when in 1787 the Grand Lodge of England legalized its existence by granting it a charter direct from the "fountain-head," while Boston Lodge received its charter from a Provincial Grand Master only? We think so.

Our second witness is St. Andrew's Lodge, which formed the basis of the present Grand Lodge of Massachusetts, and whose Centennial was celebrated in Boston, in 1856, and again in 1869. This is such a bad case of irregularity, that we wonder how any intelligent Mason can permit himself to charge us with irregularity, without calling to his cheek the blush of shame. But to the facts which we cull from several sources, chief of which are the following:—Bro. Hamilton Willis' oration, delivered before St. Andrew's Lodge, November 30th, 1856; Bro. C. W. Moore's oration, delivered December 23, 1869; and Brother Gardner's address, delivered December 27, 1869. In 1738, owing to differences among the Masons of Great Britain, a large body of Masons seceded from the Grand Lodge of England, and soon after established a rival Grand Body. The English Grand Lodge, in order to distinguish its adherents from the seceders introduced a test, which act the seceders denounced as an innovation and immediately styled the Old Grand Lodge as "Moderns," and themselves as "Ancients." As a consequence, the English-speaking craft was divided into two factions, which was not confined alone to Great Britain, but extended to its colonies. The records show that in 1752 there were residing in Boston a number of Masons who did not recognize the authority of the Grand Lodge of England, neither did they yield obedience to the St. John's Grand Lodge of Massachusetts. They termed themselves "Ancients," and proceeded to form a Lodge *in accordance with immemorial usage* prior to 1721. This action was called into question by St. John's Grand Lodge, and denounced as being irregular. The immediate cause of this organization was the fact that the participants therein had previously made efforts to visit the St. John's Grand Lodge, but as they were known as "Ancients," and as the Grand Lodge of England, from which St. John's derived its authority, had already declared these "Ancients" as being "irregular" and "clandestine," they were refused admittance. Smarting under this rebuff, without the authority of either a military Lodge, a local Lodge, a dispensation, or a warrant, but only upon the authority of "*immemorial usage*" prior to 1721, they proceeded to establish a Lodge with a membership composed of one "James Logan, and a number of Masons, many of whom had been made in foreign countries." *There is no record to show in what Lodges, when, or where they were made Masons.* One authority, Brother Gardner, of Massachusetts, says: "They were made Masons after the ancient system in some irregular way." In 1754 they forwarded a petition to the Grand Lodge of Scotland for a charter. It received the approval of the Committee in 1756, but was not made out for four years thereafter. It was received in Boston, September 4th, 1760.

Let us see what was done in the meantime by this Lodge formed "*in accordance with immemorial usage:*"

"George Bray was initiated in 1753, whose name was afterwards inserted in the charter. On the 3d of April, 1758, four were 'raised,' and several—at least six—were made Masons, and still their charter did not reach Boston."

Now we ask all unprejudiced minds to compare the Prince Hall organization from 1775 to 1787 with St. Andrew's organization from 1752 to 1760. The Prince Hall organization could at least trace the Masonic origin of its members, establish their legality, and present some show of authority; furthermore, it has never been charged, or even hinted at, that the Prince Hall organization attempted to do any Masonic work during this period. The most that has been said is that they met together in a social way to devise plans for their future benefit, which culminated in their asking and receiving a charter from the Grand Lodge of England. Was this the case with the St. Andrew's Lodge ? No. From 1752 to 1760, they met in Lodge capacity without any authority, and entered, passed, and raised Masons—as clear a case of illegality and irregularity as was ever presented to the Masonic world. Yet this Lodge furnished to the Massachusetts Grand Lodge its first Provincial Grand Master, Bro. Joseph Warren, of Bunker Hill fame. Yet this Lodge—St. Andrew's Lodge, No. 82, Scotch Registry—was the chief corner stone of the Massachusetts Grand Lodge which to-day charges African Lodge, No. 459 with irregularity. And yet again, in 1856 and 1869, the white Masons of Massachusetts, clad in holiday array, celebrated two Centennials—the first, commemorative of the granting of a warrant to a body of men, known throughout the land as illegal and irregular; the second, commemorative of the organization of a Grand Lodge whose chief constituent Lodge was this same illegal and irregular body. For shame, for shame, that men would be so blind to truth and justice as to celebrate that which they know to have been illegal and spurious, and spurn that which they know is legal and pure, because the skin of one is white while that of the other is black !

These St. Andrew's Masons were unable to obtain any recognition from the St. John's Grand Lodge, although they made frequent applications and piteously begged for the same. Their irregularity was too well established, although, in our opinion, St. John's Grand Lodge was very little better, if any. In order that you may know how they (St. Andrew's) were regarded at that time, we quote from the " memorial address" of Bro. C. W. Moore, of Massachusetts, on the occasion of the Centennial of Massachusetts Grand Lodge, 1869:

"1776, 27th of January, St. John's Lodge rebuffed St. Andrew's, which made a formal tender to receive officers and members at their lodge-room whenever it may be agreeable to them, and that there may be '*a happy* coalition.'

"The rebuff was in four votes:

'1. Claiming that the nine persons (naming them) who were the only ones named as Masons in the charter to Lodge of St. Andrew's, *were not at the date of their application for it, or at the date of Constitution, Free and Accepted Masons.*—[Italics ours.]

'2. That applying as such was an imposition on the Grand Lodge of Scotland.

'3. That they are irregular Masons, and all persons who have since been added to them in their fraternity. [This included Dr. Joseph Warren, made in the Scotch Lodge, 1761.]

'4. That, as members of such irregular Lodge, some attempting to visit their regular Lodges had been refused this liberty, and that by vote of the Grand Lodge visit of their members to said irregular Lodge has been prohibited.

'Therefore, this answer is given to written request for us to visit your Lodge, that the Free and Accepted Masons under this jurisdiction can not visit said fraternity.'

"These were sent to St. Andrew's, also to Grand Lodge, England.'"

This is the verdict rendered against St. Andrew's Lodge by the Masons who were on the ground at the time of its organization. It is not of record that any such verdict was ever rendered against the Prince Hall Masons, excepting that rendered by the white Masons of America, within the last three or four decades, and that upon such a shallow basis that under the pressure of historical investigation it has crumbled to dust. The hope of the white American Mason for our continued rejection hangs upon one slender thread, "exclusive territorial jurisdiction," and if he will be convinced by sound logic, he must even see that disappear.

The white Masonic historians, knowing of the many irregularities of their early organization, seek many ways to find excuses and make apologies for them. In this connection Bro. C. W. Moore apologizes for the irregularity of St. Andrew's Lodge as follows:

"The validity of the charter of the Lodge and the lawful making of the petitioners for it were matters in which the *Grand Lodge* [St. John's] *had no control or right to interfere. Both subjects had passed beyond its reach.* Whatever may have been irregular in the proceedings of the Lodge in the earlier days of its organization *had been Masonic-*

ally regularized and confirmed by the Grand Lodge of Scotland, under whose authority it existed, and to which body it was alone amenable. If the St. John's Grand Lodge had any grievances to complain of, it was to that body its complaints should have been preferred."

These are true words and we fully agree with Bro. Moore, but if he had only said them, as he could and ought have done in behalf of the early organization of African Lodge, No. 459, we could then have said they have the ring of true nobility; but when he says them in behalf of his own Grand Lodge in which he has a personal interest, and at the same time stands with his foot upon the neck of African Lodge, No. 459, we can only say they are extremely selfish. Yet they are true, nevertheless, and the day must come when truth, though crushed to earth, will rise again.

We believe our two witnesses, the St. John's Lodge, of Boston, English Registry, and the St. Andrew's Lodge, of Boston, Scotch Registry, have fully proven our proposition, which is, if, according to Bro. Gardner, dispensations were not made use of in the early days as preliminary to granting charters, that if we can find any body of white Masons that assembled as a Lodge without any documentary authority to do so, and which has subsequently been received and acknowledged as a just and legal Lodge of Masons, then must all objection to African Lodge, No. 459, on these grounds fall. That St. John's and St. Andrew's Lodges came under these conditions is fully established. Therefore, African Lodge, No. 459, is entitled to the same recognition.

We digress one moment to say that we think Bro. Gardner is mistaken when he says, "dispensations for Lodges, as preliminary to granting a charter, were not made use of in those days." We know of one Lodge that never had a charter until it became a part of the Grand Lodge of Ohio, and then not for some time after its connection therewith. We refer to American Union Lodge. Here is the record:

"The meetings of the Grand Lodge having been suspended, application was made to the Hon. John Rowe, Grand Master, for a *dispensation*, which he was pleased to grant to Joel Clark, Esq., one of the petitioners, appointing and constituting him Master of the American Union Lodge," etc., etc.

The dispensation is dated February 15, 1776, and is signed by the Deputy Grand Master and the Junior Grand Warden only.

Were it necessary we could cite other examples; but more of this further on.

We believe that Prince Hall had some form of written authority certifying to the fact that he and his associates were legally made Masons, and empowering them to meet and act as such. Prince Hall being a leader among his people, as is attested by the many public addresses made by him, and the many memorials addressed to the Legislative bodies of that period to which his signature was always attached, and knowing the value of documentary evidence, the pre- sumption is, that he secured from the Army Lodge in which he was made some documentary proof of the same, and no doubt this accompanied their petition for a charter. But Grand Master Gardner says, "but more than all, there was no authorized power here to grant such dispensations, save Provincial Grand Masters Rowe aud Warren. A traveling Lodge, though attached to a British regiment, could not authorize these persons to assemble as a Lodge."

We agree with Bro. Gardner this far : That such Lodges as were subordinate to the Provincial Grand Lodges over which Grand Masters Rowe and Warren had authority could exist legally only by virtue of dispensations granted by them, or by warrants subsequently granted by the mother Grand Lodge from which the Provincial Grand Masters derived their authority. I think historical research will prove that military or traveling Lodges frequently granted authority to Masons to meet in the capacity of Lodges. Let us see. Bro. Jacob Norton, of Massachusetts, in his "Additional Facts and Suggestions concerning the Ancients," says as follows :

" In my reply to Mackey on the colored question, I expressed my belief that a notion prevailed in the last century that a Lodge had a right to grant a dispensation for the formation of a new Lodge ; that Prince Hall, no doubt, received such a dispensation from the Army Lodge, and therefore he thought it proper to grant similar documents to the colored brethren in Philadelphia and in Providence, R. I. Now in Bro. Brennan's ' History of Freemasonry in British America,' I found two letters copied from the originals preserved in the archives at Halifax. The first dated November 7; 1783 (St. Ann's, New Brunswick). An army officer, whose regiment was disbanded, but who was still in possession of an Irish Army charter, asked Bro. J. Peters, Secretary of a Lodge at Halifax, whether he could not open a Lodge at St. Ann's under the said army charter, to which he received the following reply :

" ' It seems to be the opinion here that no objection can be made to your meeting and conversing under your old warrant, but that it will not be right, as it was granted for another province and to a regiment which is now disbanded, to proceed to making, etc., under it. We have not yet a Provincial Grand warrant here, but one is applied for, and by a late account from a brother in England we have reason to expect it daily. · When it arrives you will have regulations sent to you. Our worthy Bro. George Pyke, Esq., at present Master of St. John's Lodge, is the Provincial Grand Master elect. In the meantime I am ordered to acquaint you that *you may at any time have from the Lodges here a dispensation which will answer all the ends of a warrant,*' etc.

·" This is very significant. It shows that our notions of Masonic jurisprudence differ from the notions of the last century. Nay, more; they even then differed from each other, for, while *Prince Hall's dispensation* [this would indicate that there is evidence somewhere that Prince Hall had a dispensation] restricted the Lodge from taking new members before they received a regular warrant, the then Halifax brethren believed that the dispensation granted by their Lodges would *answer all ends of a warrant,* which means that they could initiate, pass, and raise under it."

This seems to be strong evidence that it was customary for Lodges to grant dispensations. However, we offer another quotation from Bro. John Dove's History of the Grand Lodge of Virginia, page 60 :·

"We have also evidence from the records of Falmouth Lodge, in Stafford County, that in the absence of a warrant from any Grand Lodge, the competent number of Master Masons being met and agreed, acted under this immemorial usage, only asking the nearest Lodge in writing, and which document operated as their warrant, as will be seen by the records of Fredericksburg Lodge, No. 4, in granting this privilege to the Masons in Falmouth. We are also justified in inferring that the military traveling Lodges may have in many instances imparted the degrees of Masonry to persons of respectability residing at or near their place of encampment, and on leaving gave them a warrant to confer these degrees on others in lieu of a certificate of enrollment."

We do not wish to pursue this farther as we believe we have proven to the full satisfaction of any unprejudiced person, that Prince Hall and his associates had a legal right to exist as an organized body from 1775 to 1787, and if we have not, we then rely upon the legalizing power of the Grand Lodge of England, which issued to him and his associates a charter constituting them into a just and legal Lodge of Free and Accepted Masons.

4. That no warrant was ever received from England; that what ·purported to be one was a forged, falsified document.

This objection has been so frequently refuted that it is scarcely worth while to take time in proving its falsity. Yet, that our argument may be complete we present the proof.

Prince Hall and his associates, desiring to become a part of the

Masonic family of the State in which they resided, made application to the Massachusetts Grand Lodge for a warrant of constitution. How was their request treated? Did the progeny of the May Flower Pilgrims, who came to America to escape oppression, extend to them the fraternal hand? Did they say come with us and be of us, we whose tenets are brotherly love, relief, and truth; we whose creed is the "fatherhood of God and the brotherhood of man;" we who have shed our blood, "pledged our lives, our fortunes, and our sacred honors" in support of the declaration, "All men are created equal?" No! they cast them off; they rejected them as being unfit for the building; they said we know ye not, ye can not enter in at our gates. This is no rhetorical flight. It is a fact, and we cite the *New York Dispatch* as evidence. This paper was edited by Past Grand Master Holmes, and also by Past Grand Master Simons, of New York, who is especially known for his unfavorable disposition toward the colored people. The issue of March 1, 1868, says:

"In the beginning of the eighties of last century, a number of colored people of Boston, Massachusetts, addressed the Grand Lodge of this city (Boston), requiring a dispensation to do open and work a Lodge. *This request was refused,* upon which the petitioners addressed the Grand Lodge of England, and their request was complied with."

Meeting with the refusal did not discourage Prince Hall, but with devotion to that valuable Masonic lesson, "Time, patience, and perseverance will accomplish all things," he approached the fountain head of Masonic authority—the Grand Lodge of England—and in the following language prayed for a warrant: "I would inform you that this Lodge hath been founded almost eight years. We have had no opportunity to apply for a warrant before now, though we have been importuned to send to France for one, yet we thought it best to send to the fountain head from whence we received the light for a warrant." The date of this letter is March 7, 1784.

On the 29th day of September, 1784, the Grand Lodge for the Society of Free and Accepted Masons, whose Grand East is in London, England, granted this prayer by issuing to these fifteen black men who had been spurned by the Massachusetts Grand Lodge the following

WARRANT OF CONSTITUTION
𝔄. 𝔊. 𝔐.

TO ALL AND EVERY:

Our right worshipful and loving brethren :—We, THOMAS HOWARD, Earl of Effingham, Lord Howard, etc., Acting Grand Master, under the authority of his Royal Highness, Henry Frederick, Duke of Cumberland, etc., Grand Master of the Most Ancient and Honorable Society of Free and Accepted Ancient Masons, send greeting:

Know ye that we, at the humble petition of our Right Trusty and well beloved brethren, Prince Hall, Boston Smith, Thomas Sanderson, and several other brethren residing in Boston, New England, in North America, do hereby constitute the said brethren into a regular Lodge of Free and Accepted Masons, under the title or denomination of the African Lodge, to be opened in Boston, aforesaid, and do further, at their said petition and of the great trust and confidence reposed in every of the said above-named brethren, hereby appoint the said Prince Hall to be Master; Boston Smith, Senior Warden; and Thomas Sanderson, Junior Warden, for opening the said Lodge, and for such further time only as shall be thought by the brethren thereof, it being our will that this, our appointment of the above officers, shall in no wise affect any future election of officers of said Lodge, but that such election shall be regulated, agreeable to such By-laws of the said Lodge as shall be consistent with the Grand Laws of the society, contained in the Book of Constitutions; and we hereby will, and require of you, the said Prince Hall, to take special care that all and every, the said brethren, are to have been regularly made Masons, and that they do observe, perform, and keep all the rules and orders contained in the Book of Constitutions; and, further, that you do from time to time cause to be entered, in a book kept for that purpose, an account of your proceedings in the Lodge, together with all such Rules, Orders, and Regulations as shall be made for the good government of the same, that in no wise you omit once in every year to send to us, or our successors, Grand Masters, or Rowland Holt, Esq., our Deputy Grand Master, for the time being, an account of your said proceeding, and copies of all such Rules, Orders, and Regulations as shall be made as aforesaid, together with the list of the members of the Lodge, and such sum of money as may suit the circumstances of the Lodge, and reasonably be expected toward the Grand Charity.

Moreover, we will, and require of you, the said Prince Hall, as soon as conveniently may be, to send an account in writing of what may be done by virtue of these presents.

{ Seal. }   Given at London, under our hand and seal of Masonry, this 29th day of September, A. L. 5784, A. D. 1784, by the Grand Master's command.

R. HOLT, *Deputy Grand Master.*

Attest : WILLIAM WHITE, *Grand Secretary.*

RECEIPT OF PAYMENT.

Received, 28th of February, 1787, of Captain James Scott, five pounds, fifteen shillings, sixpence, being the fees on the Warrant of Constitution for the African Lodge at Boston.

For the Grand Lodge of the Society of Free and Accepted Masons,
£5, 15s., 6d.　　　　　WILLIAM WHITE, *Grand Secretary.*

In addition to the receipt of payment for the Warrant, we offer, as further confirmation, the following extract from a letter written by Bro. John Hervey, Grand Secretary of the United Grand Lodge of England, to Charles W. Moore, Esq., Deputy Grand Master Grand Lodge of Massachusetts:

"FREEMASONS' HALL, London, W. C., 11th Nov., 1868.
"DEAR SIR AND R. W. BROTHER:—I am in receipt of your favor of the 29th ult., making enquiries respecting a Warrant granted in 1784, to a certain 'Prince Hall.' I have caused a most diligent search to be made in our books here, and the only reference that I can find is in the calendar for 1785, when a Lodge appears to have been working under the English Constitution, at Boston, under the No. 459, and called the 'African Lodge.' It afterwards became 370."

Further evidence is shown in the following letter written May 5th, 1870, by Brother Hervey, Grand Secretary of the Grand Lodge of England, to Brother Gardner, Grand Master of Massachusetts:

"M. W. SIR AND BROTHER:—　.　.　.　As you are already aware, the Warrant for the African Lodge was granted in 1784, and was numbered 459; but the fee for the Warrant does not appear in our Grand Lodge accounts until the 4th of April, 1787. The following remittances were received for the Charity Fund from the African Lodge, viz:

November 25, 1789 . . . . £2 2s. 11d.
April 18, 1792 . . . . 1 1 0
November 27, 1793 . . . . 1 5 6
November 22, 1797 . . . . 1 5 0

"In 1793 its number was altered to 370, and continued so numbered in our calendar until 1812, when, on the re-numbering consequent on the union of the two Grand Lodges, the African Lodge, was ommitted.

"I send you enclosed a verbatim copy of all the documents I can discover relating to the Lodge."—[Grand Lodge Proc., Mass., 1870, p. 47.]

The "documents" above referred to consist partly of correspondence between Prince Hall and William White, Esq., Grand Secretary of the Grand Lodge of England, in which Prince Hall informs the Grand Secretary of work done in African Lodge, of money sent for the Charity Fund, of the condition of the craft, etc., etc. One of these letters, written in answer to inquiries made concerning other Lodges (white) in New England from which no tidings had been received for a long time, I give in full:

"August 20, 1792.

"WORSHIPFUL BROTHER:—I received yours of the 20th of August last, with the printed accounts of the state of the Grand Lodge, and am happy to see the flourishing state of the society, and am very sorry to see so many Lodges whose behavior hath been such as to put the Grand Lodge to so disagreeable a task as to erase them from so honorable a society [probably some of the American Lodges]. I have made inquiry about the Lodges you wrote me about. The Lodge No. 42, which used to meet at the Royal Exchange and kept at the Assembly House at the head of Orange Tree Lane, has kept a regular Lodge, and was joined last year by one or two more Lodges. Their present Grand Master is John Cutler, chosen last year, and walked to Trinity Church, where a sermon was delivered by the Rev. Walter, D. D., June 25th. The Lodge No. 88 hath joined the above Lodge ever since the death of their Grand Master, Henry Price, Esq., for he is long since dead—a worthy Mason.

"As for the Marble Head Lodge, No. 91, I can not get any information of it whether it keeps or not, but I believe they don't, for if they did I should have heard from her. As for the Lodge No. 93, in New Haven, Conn., I hear they keep a regular Lodge, and I have reason to believe it. The Lodge No. 142 do keep the same, *as some of them hath visited our Lodge*, and heard it from their own mouths. I am happy you approve the sermon. I have sent you a charge I delivered at Charlestown, on the 25th of June last. I have sent one to your Royal Grand Master, His Royal Highness, the Prince of Wales, and another to his deputy, and three for the Grand Lodge, which I hope will meet your approval.

"(Signed.)   PRINCE HALL."

As further evidence we submit the following clipping from "Massachussets Centinal," printed at Boston, and which we find in Grand Lodge Proceedings of Massachussets, 1870. It is from the issue of May 2, 1787, and is in the nature of an official communication:

"AFRICAN LODGE, Boston, May 2, 1787.

"By Captain Scott, from London, came the charter, etc., which his Royal Highness, the Duke of Cumberland, and the Grand Lodge have been graciously pleased to grant to the African Lodge in Boston. As the brethren have a desire to acknowledge all favors shown them, they, in this public manner, return particular thanks to a certain number of the fraternity, who offered the so generous reward in this paper some time since, for the charter supposed to be lost, and to assure him, though they doubt of his friendship, that he has made them many good friends.

"(Signed.)   PRINCE HALL."

In 1869 the colored Masons of Massachusetts presented a petition to the Grand Lodge of Massachusetts (white) praying for recognition. A committee was appointed on the same, and a part of their report was as follows: "Your committee have examined this charter [the original charter from England], and believe it to be authentic." [See Grand Lodge Proceedings, Massachusetts, 1869.]

It seems to us that the foregoing documentary evidence is sufficient to convince any one, let him be as prejudiced as he may, that a warrant was granted in 1784 to Prince Hall and his associates; that it was received in this country in 1787; that it was not a forged, falsified document; that it was not returned to England, but was as late as 1869 seen in this country by reputable witnesses. The fact that Prince Hall was in correspondence with the Grand Secretary of England, and was inquired of concerning the white Lodges in this country, and the further fact that moneys were sent by Prince Hall to the charity fund, in accordance with the requirements of the charter, at various times from 1789 to 1797, and were receipted for and acknowledged by the Grand Secretary of England, and the still further fact that when the Lodges on the English registry were renumbered in 1793 African Lodge was also renumbered, is conclusive proof that African Lodge was known to the Grand Lodge of England as a legal and regular Lodge in working order, at least as late as 1797. That is more, very much more, than can be said of many white Lodges that formed a constituent part of some of the Grand Lodges that are loudest in their charges of dormancy and consequent loss of life against us.

We pass to the fifth objection:

5. That if received it was returned to England for correction, but never again received in America, a mutilated copy being used in its stead.

That it was received we think is proved; that it was returned to England for correction there is not the slightest evidence. The only fact that might be so construed is a letter, which may be found in the proceedings of the Grand Lodge of Massachusetts for 1870, addressed " *To the Right Worshipful, the Grand Master Wardens, and members of the Grand Lodge of England,*" and dated at Boston, January 5, 1824, "praying that, in addition to the warrant granted to Prince Hall and his associates in 1784, under which they could confer but three degrees, a new warrant be granted to the petitioners authorizing them to confer seven degrees." The petitioners were sufficiently careful, as subsequent events have shown, to retain the original warrant. Even had

they sent it, and never again received it, they would have lost nothing
but a valuable relic; for long before this time, 1824, legal Grand
Lodges had been established, with as full power and authority to grant
warrants and institute new Lodges as any white Grand Lodge that had
been established in America.

With regard to a mutilated copy being used in its stead we have to
say, that Bro. C. W. Moore, of Massachusetts, who persisted for many
years in making this statement, did, in 1869, report to the Grand
Lodge of Massachusetts that the warrant was an authentic document.
However, we believe that, if only a "mutilated copy" had been used,
it would have been as regular and as legal for African Lodge, No.
459 to use it as for any of the white Lodges under Massachusetts Grand
Lodge to do similarly. You ask did any of them do so? We say, yes.
Here is the record, which you will find in proceedings of Massachusetts, 1870:

"St. John's Lodge, first Lodge in Boston; no written charter
until one was granted by Provincial Grand Master Rowe. This charter was burnt in Winthrop House fire. A copy of the charter was
furnished by the Grand Officers in 1864, which copy bears date of
February 7, 1783. *Much doubt exists as to the accuracy of this copy.*"

We deem this one example sufficient to sustain our statement;
others may be found in the record.

6. That, if a warrant were granted them, it was in violation of the
territorial rights of the Massachusetts Grand Lodge.

Somewhere in the foregoing may be found the proof that a warrant
was granted; therefore, it is not necessary to reiterate.

With regard to the violation of the territorial rights of the Massachusetts Grand Lodge, we will say in brief that the Massachusetts
Grand Lodge had no territorrial rights to violate when the Grand
Lodge of England granted warrant No. 459 to African Lodge. We
reserve the discussion of this point until we reach the "thirteenth
objection."

7. That if they were legally warranted it was only as a subordinate
Lodge, and that it was an assumption of authority on the part of Prince
Hall to establish Lodges in Philadelphia and Providence, Rhode
Island; and that the Grand Lodge established in Boston, in 1808, with
African Lodge, No. 459, and the Lodges in Philadelphia and Provi-
dence was an irregular body, and as a consequence all its descent is
illegal and clandestine.

That they were legally warranted is fully established, and we are willing to admit that it was as a subordinate Lodge. But even this does not affect the subsequent establishment of Lodges in Philadelphia and Providence, Rhode Island. In the preceding we quoted from Bro. Jacob Norton, and from Bro. Dove, Grand Secretary of Virginia, to show that it was a matter of frequent occurence for a subordinate Lodge, or a military traveling Lodge to issue authority to Masons to assemble as a Lodge and do work therein. Prince Hall was evidently cognizant of these customs, and believing himself to have full power to do so, he assembled the brethren in Philadelphia and Providence, and organized them into Lodges. And while we have no documentary evidence that Prince Hall was a deputized Provincial Grand Master, yet we have strong presumptive evidence that he was so recognized by the English authorities. This is inferred from the title of Right Worshipful, by which he was addressed by the Grand Secretary of England, and also from the fact that special inquiry was made of him concerning the Lodges here, indicating that a more than ordinary trust was reposed in him. If, however, Prince Hall had none of the powers of a Provincial Grand Master, because of the absence of any documentary proof of the same, then must the same be said of Henry Price, the first Provincial Grand Master (white) of Massachusetts, for there is no record of his appointment as such in 1733. The earliest appointment shown by the records of the Grand Lodge of England is for Robert Tomlinson in 1736. Now, if the acts of Henry Price, without a deputation, were regular, so then were those of Prince Hall. Therefore the Grand Lodge, established in 1808 with African Lodge, No. 459, and the Lodges at Philadelphia and Providence, was as much a legal Grand Lodge as the one established by Henry Price and known as St. John's Grand Lodge.

To strengthen this point we desire now to give the details of the organization of two or three white Grand Lodges, some of whom have celebrated their centennials, and compare them with the African Grand Lodge established in 1808.

According to general acceptation, not sustained by records, Henry Price received from the Grand Master of England, in 1733, a deputation as Provincial Grand Master of North America. He appointed several brethren as Provincial Grand Officers, and on July 30, 1733, organized the St John's Grand Lodge. Let us see how this Grand Lodge was organized. First, we quote from Mackey's Jurisprudence several paragraphs relating to the "Nature of a Grand Lodge" of the form introduced in 1717, and followed generally from that time until the present:

"Lodges are the aggregations of Masons as individuals in their primary capacity. Grand Lodges are the aggregations of subordinate Lodges in their representative capacity." (P. 406.)

"Lenning defines a Grand Lodge to be the 'dogmatic and administrative authority of several particular Lodges of a country or province which is usually composed of the Grand Officers and of the Presiding Officers of these particular Lodges.'" (P. 407.)

Concerning the organization of a Grand Lodge, Mackey says, on page 423, *Masonic Jurisprudence:* "In the first place, it is essential that not less than three Lodges shall unite in forming a Grand Lodge."

Now when Henry Price organized the St. John's Grand Lodge, of Massachusetts, he not only did not have three Lodges, but he did not have *one* Lodge. Upon receiving his deputation, he appointed, from among the brethren residing in Boston, several Provincial Grand Officers, and, on the next day, at the request of a number of brethren, he constituted them into a Lodge, known as St. John's Lodge. No other Lodge was instituted in Massachusetts under this authority until February 15, 1750. The third Lodge in Massachusetts was established March 17, 1750. Thus we see that the requisite number of Lodges— three—to organize a Grand Lodge had not been instituted until seventeen years after Henry Price's illegal erection of the St. John's *Grand* Lodge, first, and St. John's *Subordinate* Lodge, second. No subsequent reorganization of this Grand Lodge was ever made, but it went on granting charters until it had granted warrants to nearly forty Lodges located in the different colonies. It suspended its meetings in 1775, the last meeting being held February 27, 1775. The next meeting held was in August, 1787, for the purpose of attending the funeral of Grand Master Rowe; it met again in 1790, and elected officers, none higher than Senior Grand Warden; it also met again in 1792 to make arrangements to unite with the St. Andrew's Grand Lodge, one of its acts being to elect a Grand Master, there not having been any since the death of Grand Master Rowe, in 1787. Its existence terminated March 5, 1792, at which time it united with the St. Andrew's Grand Lodge to form the present Grand Lodge of Massachusetts. Your attention is called to the fact that the new Grand Lodge, formed in 1792, adopted the ritual as worked by the St. John's Grand Lodge, and also elected for their Grand Master the same brother chosen by the St. John's Grand Lodge a short time before the union; and all this, notwithstanding Bro. Gardner's assertion, that "it is evident that the St. John's Grand Lodge preserved its organization as such only for the purpose of completing the contemplated union. It granted no charters, nor did it assume any of the powers of a Grand Lodge." A strange thing, we would say, to see a Grand Lodge preserve its organization as such for the purpose of completing the contemplated union, to see it go into the union and form a part of the new Grand Lodge, to see its ritual adopted, and to see its Grand Master chosen as the Grand Master of the United Grand Lodge, and yet, all this time, according to Bro. Gardner, not assuming any of the powers of a Grand Lodge! We know why Bro. Gardner made this statement. We will refer to it when we come to the subject of Exclusive Territorial Jurisdiction. Now, then, we reiterate our proposition, made at the commencement of this topic, which is, that the Lodges formed by Prince Hall, and the resultant Grand Lodge, were as regular and as legal as the St. John's Grand Lodge, formed by Henry Price without any Lodge, and, moreover, without any authority, so far as the records show. We say this for two reasons: First, because his acts were in accordance with the usages of that period, as shown by the quotations already made from Bros. Norton and Dove; secondly, because on page 27, vol. ii, of the *American Freemason*, April 18, 1869, may be found the following:

"On the call for papers, by a Commission of the Grand Lodge of Massachusetts, it has been proven that Prince Hall was duly appointed Provincial Grand Master for Lodges of black men in America, by exactly the same English Grand Lodge which appointed Henry Price, sixty years previously, a Provincial Grand Master for Lodges of white men in America; and that he was corresponded with by the authorities of such English Grand Lodge, and recognized in that official capacity as long as was any other English-appointed Grand Master for any portion of the United States."

In further support of the regularity of the Prince Hall Grand Lodge, as well as Prince Hall's authority to act as a Provincial Grand Master, we submit the opinions and conclusions of eminent white Masonic scholars concerning the same, and some of whom we know to be unfriendly toward us.

Bro. Robbins, in his report to the Grand Lodge of Illinois, in 1876, says:

"We believe, and we think we have shown in former reports, that the original legitimacy of African Lodge, out of which the Prince Hall Grand Lodge grew, is beyond question; and that its members were robbed of their just rights when the Grand Lodge of Massachusetts was formed in 1792."

In answer to a letter written by Bro. John D. Caldwell, Grand Secretary of the Grand Lodge of Ohio, and editor of "*New Day—New*

Duty," to Ill. ∴ Bro. Albert Pike, asking his opinion on the Masonic regularity of the Prince Hall Lodges of men of color, Bro. Pike, under date of 13th September, 1875, Alexandria, Va., replied as follows:

" Our folks only *stave off* the question by saying that negro Masons here are clandestine. Prince Hall Lodge was as regular a Lodge as any Lodge created by competent authority, and had a perfect right (as other Lodges in Europe did) to establish other Lodges, making itself a mother Lodge. That's the way the Berlin Lodges—Three Globes and Royal York—became Grand Lodges."

Bro. Theodore S. Parvin, whom Bro. John D. Caldwell compliments as being one of the best informed Masonic officers in any of the States, in answer to the same inquiry, writes as follows:

" I have read opinions of Pike and Lewis in the pamphlet you sent me. My opinion is that the negroes can make as good a show for the legality of their Grand Lodges as the whites can. It is only a matter of taste, and not of laws.

" I am satisfied that all the world outside the United States will, ere long, recognize them, and I think we had much better acknowledge them than to blend them into our organizations."

Grand Master Griswold in his address to the Grand Lodge of Minnesota, has the following, with much other excellent matter that we much desire to quote, to say:

" After a somewhat careful investigation of this matter, I am satisfied that the so called irregularities attending the organization of the first colored Grand Lodge in this country were fewer in number and of less importance than those pertaining to some other American Grand Lodges—Grand Lodges, now venerable with age, to whom we look with feelings of reverence, who have been mighty powers in giving tone to American Masonry—who stand to-day deservedly in the lead, and from whom we trace our Masonic descent. The facts are, brethren, that with reference to these matters we are 'living in glass houses,' and it is not, in my opinion, at all wise for us to engage in the sport of throwing stones."

With the opinions of such eminent Masonic scholars as these in our favor we think the legitimacy of Prince Hall Grand Lodge is well established.

But we desire to briefly state the facts connected with the organization of two or three other Grand Lodges.

First, the St. Andrew's Grand Lodge, or Massachusetts Grand Lodge. The chief constituent Lodge, St. Andrew's, "originated in 1752 *by nine clandestine made Masons.* In 1756, when it was chartered by the Grand Lodge of Scotland, it numbered twenty-one members, exclusive of one of the original nine, who left Boston in the interval. Its charter did not arrive until 1760, at which time the Lodge had been increased by eighteen additional members; so that in all thirty-one candidates were initiated before the Lodge received its charter, and thirteen before the charter was signed."—[Robbins, Ill., 1871]. In 1769, St. Andrew's, with three Army Lodges, formed the Massachusetts Grand Lodge, with Joseph Warren as Grand Master. In 1775, Bro. Warren was killed at the battle of Bunker Hill. According to Bro. Gardner's exposition of the powers of a Provincial Grand Lodge, and also a Provincial Grand Master, when Provincial Grand Master Joseph Warren expired on Bunker Hill, June 17, 1775, the Provincial Grand Lodge of which he was the essence and life, expired also, and with it all the officers of which it was composed. In 1777, February 14th, a Grand Lodge was called by the deputy of Warren to hear the petition of a number of brethren for a charter; they doubted their power to act and called another meeting for the 7th of March, to which all Masters and Wardens were summoned by the Deputy Grand Master. Now, if Bro. Gardner's conclusions were correct, by what authority could the Deputy call a Grand Lodge meeting? What authority had he to summon any one? None whatever. Let us see what was the result of this summons. On the 8th of March eleven brethren answered the summons, and "proceeded to unanimously elect a Grand Master, Grand Wardens, and other grand officers, Joseph Webb being chosen Grand Master." We here quote Brother Gardner's requirement for a Grand Lodge organization: "Three regularly chartered Lodges existing in any State or Territory have the right to establish a Grand Lodge." We will now see if such was the case in the re-organization in 1777. There were present, the Master of St. Peter's Lodge, the Senior Warden and seven other members of St. Andrew's Lodge, a Past Master and one other member of Tyrian Lodge, making eleven in all, only two of whom could be considered representative officers in any sense of the term; therefore only two Lodges were represented instead of three, as Brother Gardner states is necessary. Please do not forget the fact that when Prince Hall Grand Lodge was organized in 1808, there were three Lodges represented. Yet this organization is the basis of the Grand Lodge which characterizes the Prince Hall Grand Lodge as being irregular.

We will now call your attention to the organization of the Grand Lodge of New Hampshire. We are indebted to Brother Gardner, of

Massachusetts, for this scrap of history. Brother Bell, of New Hampshire, from the "Committee on Foreign Correspondence," in reviewing Massachusetts in 1869 on the topic of the violation of the territorial rights of Massachusetts in the establishment of African Lodge, No. 459, says:

"In Massachusetts there was no legal Grand Lodge until the union in 1792."

This stirs up Brother Gardner, as it were, with a sharp stick, and he replies to Brother Bell in his memorable address of 1870, which is so rich in valuable historical matter relating to negro Masonry. Brother Gardner says:

"The Grand Lodge of New Hampshire was organized on the 8th of July, 1789, by four deputies from St. John's Lodge of Portsmouth, chartered by Massachusetts 'St. John's Grand Lodge,', June 24th, 1734, and one deputy from Rising Sun Lodge, of Keene, chartered by the Massachusetts Grand Lodge, March 5, 1784—five deputies from two Lodges. All Masonic authorities claim that to organize a legitimate Grand Lodge, there must be present the representatives of not less than three Lodges holding charters or warrants from some legal Grand Lodge."

We again call attention to the fact that at the organization of Prince Hall Grand Lodge in 1808 there were present the representatives of three regular Lodges. What think you of our descent as compared with Massachusetts and New Hampshire?

This is what Brother Gardner says concerning the relations existing between his own Grand Lodge and the Grand Lodge of New Hampshire, which he has shown to be so irregularly formed:

"However irregularly organized the Grand Lodge of New Hampshire may have been, the 'Massachusetts Grand Lodge' disclaimed jurisdiction in that State thereafter. It is unnecessary to state that this Grand Lodge, since 1789 to the present time, has been on the most friendly and fraternal relations with our sister Grand Lodge of New Hampshire."

What a commentary here upon the attitude of the Grand Lodge of Massachusetts towards the negro Masons of America, who can show, by the very records brought to light by her, a clearer and better title to legitimacy than either Massachusetts or New Hampshire. Does it need a seer to tell the reason of this unjust discrimination? *Shame!* SHAME!! SHAME!!!

Brother Robbins, of Illinois, in commenting upon Brother Gardner's expose of the organization of the Grand Lodge of New Hampshire, disposes of the matter so gracefully and at the same time gives Massachusetts such a hard rub that we quote him in full on this point. He says:

"All the Lodges in New Hampshire existing prior to 1790, with the single exception of St. John's, was chartered by the 'Massachusetts Grand Lodge.'

"He then shows from the records that five Lodges were chartered in New Hampshire by the 'Massachusetts Grand Lodge' during the period alluded to by Brother Bell, and remarks, 'that however irregularly organized the Grand Lodge of New Hampshire may have been, the Massachusetts Grand Lodge disclaimed jurisdiction in that State thereafter.' If it should appear that the Massachusetts Grand Lodge was no more regularly organized than the Grand Lodge of New Hampshire, this disclaimer may lose something of its apparent magnanimity and the boundary line between dangerous and safe ground have to be sought farther South than Brother Gardner intimates. He says, as we have seen, that 'all Masonic authorities claim that to organize a legitimate Grand Lodge, there must be present the representatives of not less than three Lodges holding charters or warrants from some legal Grand Lodge.' Now as it can not, by any one, be shown that the Massachusetts Grand Lodge itself complied with this dictum, we can not but think that Brother Gardner had forgotten the old proverb when he shied that bolder at our New Hampshire brethren. We think we speak advisedly when we say that there is no evidence in existence to show that a single one of the eleven brethren named by him as being present March 8, 1777, was the representative of a Lodge or authorized by any Lodge to participate in the business in which they then engaged, that of organizing a Grand Lodge. It can not be shown even that the two members of Tyrian Lodge, Gloucester, nor he of St. Peter's Lodge. Newburyport, were authorized representatives of the bodies to which they belonged.

"Eight of the eleven persons present were members of St. Andrew's Lodge, Boston. But St. Andrew's Lodge not consenting, how could it be represented? St. Andrew's Lodge did not recognize the Massachusetts Grand Lodge; did not even come under the jurisdiction of the United Grand Lodge until 1810, up to which time it worked under the authority of the Grand Lodge of Scotland and paid dues to that body; but, on the contrary, at the origin of the Massachusetts Grand Lodge, and subsequently, there was a high feud existing between St. Andrew's Lodge and that body, St. Andrew's Lodge being the thorn in its side, which furnishes a key to many of the acts of the Massachusetts Grand Lodge in those days, among them the manifesto of December 6, 1782, which was an attempt to coerce St. Andrew's Lodge into submission to it. Manifestly then the eight members of St. Andrew's Lodge present when the Massachusetts Grand Lodge was formed can not be said to have represented that Lodge.

"Of the other three persons present the most that can be said is, that there is a bare possibility that they were authorized by the two Lodges of which they were members to represent them, but of this, as we have before stated, there is absolutely no evidence.   It is admitted that the Grand Lodge of New Hampshire was formed by five deputies representating two Lodges, and it is nowhere claimed that it was reduced to the necessity of selecting its Grand Master from a Lodge which did not consent to its formation, nor recognize its authority when formed."

These are historical facts sustained by unquestioned records, and which prove beyond a doubt the irregular formation of both the Massachusetts and New Hampshire Grand Lodges.   Now, then, if the descent from these two Grand Lodges is considered legal and regular, why not the descent of Prince Hall Grand Lodge, which was formed by the representatives of three Lodges in Boston, 1808, in a legal and regular manner?   Make all the denials that you may, weave all the complications possible, yet the intelligent observer, following the threads of history, and calmly surveying all the circumstances connected with these several organizations, will come to but one conclusion, and that is, the origin and descent of the negro Mason is in every sense of the words as legal and as regular as the white American Mason.

8. That after the death of Prince Hall, in 1807, the Lodge became dormant, and had thereafter no actual existence.

There is no force in this objection, for the merest tyro in Masonic jurisprudence knows that every warrant provides for the succession of officers; therefore, Prince Hall's death would have no effect upon the life of the Lodge.   It seems to us that no intelligent Mason would dare to make this objection a test of our legality, for by so doing he would vitiate his own existence.   With the death of Prince Hall the warrant to African Lodge, No. 459, lost none of its vitality, but we all know that with the death of Warren, on Bunker Hill, the life of the Provincial Grand Lodge of Massachusetts died with him, not by any construction of law by us, but according to the law as stated by Bro. Gardner of Massachusetts, and according to the English, Irish, and Scotch Constitutions.   Even admitting that it became dormant, it had as much right to resuscitate itself in the following year for the purpose of aiding in the formation of a Grand Lodge, as did the Lodges in Massachusetts, some of which lay dormant for more than a half score of years, and as did the American Union Lodge—one of the constituent Lodges of the Grand Lodge of Ohio—which took a sleep from April 23, 1783, to June 28, 1790, upon which date it was revived, *only two* of its members, Bros. Jonathan Heart and Rufus Putnam, being present. These two brethren, with the assistance of seven other Masons, opened the Lodge in due form. The *dispensation* granted by Grand Master Rowe in 1776 was read, which, no doubt, was satisfactory, for immediately thereafter, on motion of Bro. Putnam, the seven brothers who had just assisted in opening the Lodge in due form were proposed for membership, and being balloted for they were elected to membership. As Bro. Heart and Bro. Putnam were the only members present, we have wondered if Bro. Putnam seconded his own motion, or whether Bro. Heart, who was in the chair, seconded it. We recently read a decision of one of the Grand Masters of the Grand Lodge of Ohio in which he decided that a Lodge could do no business unless at least eight of its members were present. We wonder what that Grand Master would say about the business of American Union Lodge. It is an excellent thing for American Union Lodge that Prince Hall was not its Master, for if he had been, and had done what Bro. Heart did, it would not now be a part of the Grand Lodge of Ohio, but would have its officers and members endeavoring to convince the world that it was a legal Lodge of Masons, but for some reason robbed of its rights. It makes a mighty difference as to whose ox is gored.

But after all, African Lodge, No. 459, did not become dormant after the death of Prince Hall; there is ample evidence to prove that African Lodge was in a healthy state of activity from 1807 to 1826, at least, during which time the record shows that nearly eighty persons were initiated. Quite a lively state of dormancy we would say.

9. That in 1813, upon the union of the Grand Lodges of England, African Lodge, which had been registered as No. 459, and subsequently as 370, was removed from the list, and was never after recognized by the Grand Lodge of England.

All of this we admit to be true; but being true, what effect has it upon our legal status? Was not all the white Lodges of America removed from the English registry at the same, or at an earlier date? Did this removal from the list effect their legality? If not, then by what mode of reasoning is the conclusion reached that by this removal all legality that African Lodge, No. 459, may hitherto have had was destroyed? Both white and black Lodges must rise or fall by the same logic.

We know that the Grand Lodge of England did recognize us as

late as 1797, for her records show that at that date she received from us a contribution to the Grand Charity. No white Grand Lodge can show this.

If the United Grand Lodge of England has never since recognized us, we are of the opinion that it is not because they consider us spurious, clandestine, or illegal, but because of the strength and influence of the white American Masons. England has for the time being been led to believe that we are violating the jurisdictional rights of the white American Grand Lodges. But we believe the time is not far distant when England with her usual sense of justice will take the time to thoroughly examine this question, and upon seeing the justness of our claims, as she undoubtedly will, she will extend to her black progeny here in America the fraternal hand of Brotherly Love, Relief, and Truth.

10. That by the 'Declaration of Independence' made by the African Lodge in June, 1827, its existence came to an end.

We did no more than the Massachusetts Grand Lodge did on the 6th day of December, 1782, when it, in full Grand Lodge, adopted the following resolution, and made it a part of its constitution:

"That this Lodge be hereafter known and called by the name of the 'Massachusetts Grand Lodge of Ancient Masons,' and that it is free and independent, in its government and official authority, of any other Grand Lodge or Grand Master in the Universe."

Did this declaration of independence destroy the legality, if it had any, of the Massachusetts Grand Lodge? Was its existence brought to an end by this act? We believe not. Then why should it destroy the legality of African Lodge, or terminate its existence? We demand that you measure both of us by the same rule, and we will abide the result; any other course is dishonest, unfair, and unjust.

But admit that, by this declaration, African Lodge, No. 459, did terminate its life. What effect would that have upon the status of negro Masons in America? None whatever. It would only be the extinction of one subordinate Lodge—a something that frequently occurs in every Grand Lodge jurisdiction without in the least affecting the Grand Body.

In 1827 negro Masons were not dependent upon the existence of any one subordinate Lodge, for long before then they had provided for the legal propagation of the principles of Masonry and the regular succession of its organization by the establishment of Grand Lodges in a legal and regular manner. Masonry among colored men in America was well on its way in the dissemination of those sublime principles underlying the institution of Freemasonry, and was successfully creating therefrom a superstructure which sometime, sooner or later, will be tried by the square of virtue and receive its just designation of good and true work.

11. That by the surrender of its warrant to the "National Grand Lodge," in 1847, it lost its character as a Grand Lodge.

Before meeting this objection, it will be necessary for us to know something of the nature of the organization known as the "National Grand Lodge." In 1847 there were only three colored Grand Lodges in America; viz: "African Grand Lodge of Massachusetts" (Boston), the "First Independent African Grand Lodge of North America" (Penn.), and the "Hiram Grand Lodge of Pennsylvania." The members of these organizations, believing that the interests of Masonry among colored men in America would be enhanced and better protected by placing its control in the hands of a central power, met in convention in June, 1847, and organized the "National Grand Lodge of the United States of North America," which was to be "the Supreme Masonic Power in the United States."

In other words, this National Grand Lodge became a supreme power over all the territory of the United States of America, just as England did in the early part of the last century; and the Grand Lodges that received warrants from this National Grand Lodge sustained the same relation to it as the Provincial Grand Lodges, acting under the authority of Deputations, sustained to the mother Grand Lodge in England. The objection made is, that, by the surrender of the warrant of African Lodge to the National Grand Lodge in 1847, it lost its character as a Lodge, and, consequently, ceased to exist. Now the fact is, no warrant of any subordinate Lodge was surrendered to the National Grand Lodge. The only action taken in the matter of warrants was that the Grand Lodges forming the convention should recognize the newly organized National Grand Lodge as the Supreme Masonic Authority of the United States, and agree to take out warrants as Grand Lodges subordinate thereto. The only error made was the surrender by the Grand Lodges forming the National Grand Lodge of their sovereignty as supreme Masonic authorities; the legal existence of the subordinate Lodges was in no ways disturbed, no more so than the subordinate Lodges under the Provincial Grand Lodges, which, in turn, were subordinate to the Grand Lodges of

England and Scotland. We believe the organization of the National
Grand Lodge to have been an error, but only as relating to govern-
ment, and not as to legal succession. Our white brethren endeavored
to do the same thing in 1779 and 1780, but the measure did not carry.
There is, to-day, in the United States an organization known as the
"General Grand Encampment of the United States," and, also,
another one known as the "General Grand Chapter of the United
States," both of which, to a certain extent, control the State Grand
Commanderies and State Grand Chapters. We consider both these organizations as errors in Masonic government, and we believe we are
not alone in this opinion. No doubt our white brethren have effected
these organizations for what they have deemed to be to the best interest of these departments of Masonry; to the organizers of the National
Grand Lodge we must give the same credit, and, no doubt, their idea
was borrowed from their white brethren, in whose knowledge of Masonic government they had implicit confidence. Therefore, do not
condemn us for what you have done yourselves. As we have grown
in Masonic intelligence, we have become enlightened concerning our
errors of government and have corrected them, and, to-day, the National Grand Lodge is a thing of the past, our Grand Lodges being
sovereign and supreme in their Masonic authority.

Admitting that African Lodge, No. 459, and all the other subordinate Lodges existing at that time surrendered their warrants to the new
power and received new warrants in lieu thereof, would this invalidate
the legal existence of these subordinate lodges? We think not. Is
not that the usual course in the formation of all Grand Lodges? We
have read the history of the organization of a number of white Grand
Lodges in this country, and the course of procedure after organization
was to require the subordinate Lodges to surrender their old warrants
and take out others from the new Grand Lodge.

We, therefore, claim that the validity of our organizations was not
affected, even though African Lodge did surrender its warrant. We
could, if necessary, name several white lodges in Ohio—one being in
Cincinnati and holding more than a half million dollars in real estate—
which, to-day, are not working under the warrants under which they
were first organized; these they surrendered, and took out new ones
from the Grand Lodge of Ohio. Yet does any one question the legal
succession of these Lodges, or the Grand Lodge of Ohio, which they
formed? Readers of Masonic history know that it has been the other
way; Lodges have been declared irregular, clandestine, etc., because

they would not surrender old warrants and take out new ones under a new organization, notably so in the Missouri–New Mexico imbroglio.

12. That we were not free-born, and therefore could not be made Masons, it being contrary to the ancient landmarks to do so.

In answer to this objection, we direct all those who so object to that great Bill of Rights, which the white American points to with so much pride, and which declares, "We hold these truths to be self-evident: *that* ALL MEN *are* CREATED EQUAL; *that they are* ENDOWED *by their* CREATOR *with certain* INALIENABLE RIGHTS; *that among these are* LIFE, LIBERTY, AND THE PURSUIT OF HAPPINESS."

And then we would ask, does it mean that only all white men are born equal, or that only all black men are born equal? Or does it mean what it says: "ALL MEN *are born* EQUAL?" We claim that man when born is as free as the air which God gave him to breathe; he may, by the laws and customs of his country, be deprived of his freedom after birth, but never before. The mind, that immortal part, the man himself, is free and personal, and responsible to God alone. His freedom is a birthright which man himself can never yield, because of its inalienableness, and of the exercise of which man may not justly deprive him, except as a punishment for crime.

We, of the United States of America, claim a civilization very much superior to that of the Mexican; whether it be or not we will not here attempt to decide, but we do know that the Aztec code acknowledged the absolute freedom of man at birth, whatever his condition might be after that. Prescott, in his *Conquest of Mexico*, says: "The most remarkable part of the Aztec code was that relating to slavery. The slave was allowed to have his own family. *His children were free. No one could be born to slavery in Mexico.*"

Chief Justice Holt, of the Queen's Bench, England, says:

"In England there is no such thing as a slave, and a human being never was considered a chattel to be sold for a price."

This is sufficient to show that our opinion is sustained by eminent judicial minds, and that the objection to our being free born is petty and trifling, and has no validity either in law or equity.

That it is a "landmark," which it is not in the power of man to remove, is untrue. Let us see what a "landmark" is. In "Mackey's Jurisprudence" we find the following relating to this subject:

"The foundations of Masonic law are to be found in the landmarks, or *Unwritten Law*, and in the Ancient Constitution, or the

Written Law [p. 12] : "Of the nature of the landmarks of Masonry there has been some diversity of opinion [' With respect to the landmarks of Masonry, some restrict them to the O. B., signs, tokens, and words. Others include the ceremonies of initiation, passing, and raising, and the form, dimensions, and supports; the ground, situation, and covering; the ornaments, furniture, and jewels of a Lodge, or their characteristic symbols. Some think that the order has no landmarks beyond its peculiar secrets.'—Oliver, *Dict. Symb., Mass.*], but perhaps the safest method is to restrict them to those ancient, and therefore universal customs of the order, which either gradually grew into operation as rules of action, or if it at once enacted by any competent authority were enacted at a period so remote that no account of their origin is to be found in the records of history. Both the enactors and the time of the enactment have passed away from the record, and the landmarks are therefore 'of higher antiquity than memory or history can reach.'

"The first requisite therefore of a custom or rule of action to constitute it a *landmark* is, that it must have existed from 'time whereof the memory of man runneth not to the contrary.' Its antiquity is its essential element. Were it possible for all the Masonic authorities at the present day to unite in a universal congress, and with the most perfect unanimity to adopt any new regulation, although such regulation would, so long as it remained unrepealed, be obligatory on the whole craft, yet it would not be a landmark. It would have the character of universality, it is true, but it would be wanting in that of antiquity." (P. 15.)

Now then, a few words relating to the formulation of landmarks. We have already seen that there is considerable diversity among authors as to what constitute landmarks; as a result we have, according to each author's ideas, different enumerations of landmarks. Mackey gives twenty-five landmarks as being the number; Dr. Oliver gives eight; Morris gives seventeen; Simons gives fifteen; the Constitution of the Grand Lodge of New York gives thirty-one; Mitchell gives six; Lockwood gives nineteen. We wish that we had the time and space to select from each of these authorities on Masonic law some of *their* landmarks, and show to you their utter emptiness of every essential necessary to constitute a landmark. The fact, which you will find to be so upon examination, is, many of these brethren have taken recent enactments and forms of Masonic government for their basis, and have formulated therefrom landmarks in accordance with their ideas. But as we have to do at the present time with the matter of " free-born," we will confine our examination to that point. On page 31, *Mackey's Jurisprudence*, we find :

" Landmark Eighteenth—Certain Qualifications of Candidates for

Initiation are derived from a Landmark of the Order. These qualifications are, that he shall be a man—shall be unmutilated, free-born, and of mature age. That is to say, a woman, a cripple, or a slave, or one born in slavery, is disqualified for initiation into the rites of Masonry."

Now this is a gratuitous deduction made by Mr. Mackey to sustain one of *his* landmarks. He has neither traditionary nor historical evidence to sustain his deductions. The fact is, these qualifications were nothing but regulations enacted by various Masonic assemblies, and therefore properly belonging to the general regulations, or the written law, and liable to be changed at any time that any competent Masonic authority might think it expedient to do so. And we will find by tracing the history of the regulation relating to bondmen that some Grand Lodges have thought it expedient to do so, and, I might add, justly and properly so.

In discussing the "qualifications of candidates" under the topic, "Political Qualifications," Mackey says:

"The political qualifications of candidates are those which refer to their position in society. To only one of these do any of the ancient constitutions allude. We learn from them that the candidate for the mysteries of Masonry must be 'free-born.'"

He then cites the regulations and the dates of their enactments. Please mark that Mr. Mackey refers not to a landmark, but to the ancient constitutions for his law in relation to the "qualification of candidates." Please mark again, that he gives the date of enactment and the names of the enactors, which he could not give were it a landmark, for he says, concerning landmarks, "both the enactors and the time of enactment have passed away from the record."

In the York constitutions the reason for such a regulation is given, which is a very trivial one, so much so that it has not sufficient breadth upon which to build a landmark, and therefore Mr. Mackey discourses as follows: "The reason assigned in the old York constitution for this regulation does not appear to be the correct one." Indeed! Now, if the reason was not correct, might not the statement of the regulation have been incorrect? Mr. Mackey is quite willing to accept the regulation because it suits his ideas, but he rejects the reasons; they are not strong enough to support his theories on "political qualifications." We believe that the Masons at the York Assembly knew what they were doing and assigned what they thought to be the correct reason for their actions, notwithstanding the opinion of Mr. Mackey. He gives the following as *his* reasons for its enactment:

"Slaves and persons born in servitude are not initiated, because, in the first place, as respects the former class, their servile condition renders them legally incapable of making a contract; in the second place, because the admission of slaves among freemen would be a violation of that social equality in the Lodge which constitutes one of the landmarks of Masonry; and in the third place, as respects both classes—the present slave and the freedman who was born in slavery —because the servile condition is believed to be necessarily accompanied by a degradation of mind and abasement of spirit which unfit them to be recipients of the sublime doctrines of Freemasonry."

To the first condition we have no denial to make; but it is not to the discredit of the enslaved race that it is so, but rather to the disgrace and shame of those who deprive the slave of his legal right to make a contract. Take all the comfort out of this that you may. To the other conditions we enter our protest; the statements are not philosophical; they do not agree with the principles of Masonry and are not in accord with the facts of history. We can not give further time to the discussion of this point, but we say to all those who subscribe to Mr. Mackey's "social equality" landmark, you do not understand the spirit of Masonry, and you need a new baptism; to those who subscribe to his "degradation and abasement" theory, we advise you to study the history of the enslaved nations of the earth and ascertain what has been the product of their degraded and abased minds.

If there is any faith to be placed in the traditions and history of our institution all this idle talk about "free-born" will vanish as the morning mist before the orb of day; for our institution, according to its traditions, was nurtured and fostered by a nation of bondmen and the sons of bondmen. Its rituals are based upon the incidents of an enslaved race; its culminating glory, according to its rituals, was the result of the labors of bondmen; and it was a bondman that displayed the almighty force of truth, and caused Darius to permit the building of the second Temple.

The most conclusive evidence that we have that the qualification of being free-born is simply a General Regulation which any Grand Lodge may alter or amend as it may see fit, is the action of the Grand Lodge of England, in 1838, when, by resolution, the term "free-born" was stricken from the list of "qualifications of candidates," and the word "free" inserted therefor.

Mackey says of this:

"This unwarranted innovation, which was undoubtedly a sacrifice to expediency, has met with the general condemnation of the Grand Lodges of this country."

We have no desire to comment on Mr. Mackey's opinions of this act, more than to say that the Grand Lodge of England did what she conceived to be right and in accordance with the true spirit of Masonry, while the Grand Lodges of this country, in condemning her, did what they conceived to be right and in accordance with the true spirit of prejudice against the negro.

13. That our Lodges and Grand Lodges violate the "American Doctrine of Exclusive Territorial Jurisdiction," and therefore have no legal right to exist.

This is the bulwark behind which the white American Grand Lodges are seeking refuge. If this fail them, they will indeed be in the slough of despond. Their investigating committees, and their historical committees have written letters to the Grand Lodge of England, have examined records and documents, and have made historical comparisons with the same result in every case, viz., to see all their objections met and refuted with scarcely a foot-hold left them. Bro. Gardner recognizes this fact, when, in his famous address of 1870, after examining every objection against us, he says: "This is simply a question of Grand Lodge jurisdiction, and we can consider it calmly and without prejudice." Is not this a complete and satisfactory admission in our favor? Nothing against us but the "question of Grand Lodge jurisdiction." Unless the "American Doctrine of Exclusive Territorial Jurisdiction" can be made tenable ground their case is lost.

We shall do what we can to dislodge them, and we do not feel it to be a hard task either, for precedent, custom, and law are all on our side. If we were asked to name the one thing of all others that is most damaging to the claim of the white American Grand Lodges to exclusive territorial jurisdiction, we would answer at once, the two words "American Doctrine." The assumption of this title is a direct blow at the principle of universality. One of the fundamental principles of the institution of Masonry is the universality of all its doctrines and tenets; they can no more be American than they can be European, or Asiatic, or African. And for the Grand Lodges of America to set themselves up as autocrats and institute a new doctrine is contrary to all Masonic principle, and I believe, when properly examined, will be repudiated by every Masonic power on the Globe.

The position which we take in the discussion of this question is: That no Lodge, Grand or Subordinate, holds absolute and exclusive jurisdiction over the political territory in which it is located; that two or more Lodges, Grand or Subordinate, may hold concurrent jurisdiction in the same political territory; and that the authority of each is only over the Lodges and members of its respective creation.

This being our position, we claim that the colored Grand Lodges,, with their subordinates, exercising Masonic authority in the states and territories where white Grand Lodges with their subordinates are likewise exercising Masonic authority, do not violate any Masonic principle, and therefore their legality as Grand and Subordinate bodies is not invalidated in the least.

We shall now attempt to prove the correctness of our position by well established precedent and usage, and also to prove that the American Doctrine is an assumption of authority not belonging to any Grand Lodge. To aid us in this we will adduce historical facts supplemented by the opinions of learned Masonic jurists.

We desire to notice, first, the charge that when the Grand Lodge of England granted a charter to African Lodge, No. 459, it violated the jurisdiction of the Massachusetts Grand Lodge. This we deny, for two reasons. First, on the ground that no Grand Lodge existed in Massachusetts until 1792, and we give as authority for this statement Brother Gardner, of Massachusetts. In defining the powers of a Grand Lodge, and naming the elements necessary for its constitution, he says, "Three regularly chartered Lodges existing in any State or Territory have the right to establish a Grand Lodge." Now we defy Brother Gardner or any one else to show at what time and what place "three regularly chartered Lodges" met in the State of Massachusetts and formed a Grand Lodge prior to 1792. He can not do it. History is against him. He may deduce as much as he pleases, but facts are facts, and they can not be controverted even to satisfy the claim that a legal Grand Lodge was organized in 1777. Secondly, on the ground that the Massachusetts Grand Lodge did not possess exclusive territorial jurisdiction in 1784, and, therefore, her territorial rights could not be violated. In taking this ground we admit, for the sake of argument, that the organization effected in 1777, however irregular it may have been, was a Grand Lodge, and that it continued to exercise the powers of Grand Lodge until 1782, when, not knowing whether it was a Grand Lodge or what its powers were, it "*Voted*, that a committee be appointed to draw resolutions explanatory of the powers and authority of this Grand Lodge respecting the extent and meaning of its jurisdiction, and of the exercise of any other Masonic authorities within its jurisdiction." The report of the committee was not satisfactory to all of the brethren, and as a consequence

St. Andrew's Lodge refused to sever its connection with the Grand
Lodge of Scotland, and then and there commenced an existence
subordinate to the Grand Lodge of Scotland, and independent of the
jurisdiction of the Massachusetts Grand Lodge, and remained so
until 1809. The remaining Lodges continued the organization until
1792, when the union was formed. Whatever jurisdiction the Massachusetts Grand Lodge possessed during this period—1777 to 1792—
it was certainly not exclusive; for first, there was the St. John's Grand
Lodge which commenced its existence in 1733, and possessed even
more authority to claim exclusive territorial jurisdiction than the
Massachusetts Grand Lodge, for its Provincial Grand Master was
living from 1768 to 1787, while Joseph Warren, Provincial Grand
Master of the Massachusetts Grand Lodge, died in 1775, and this
according to Brother Gardner's theories terminated the life of the
Massachusetts Grand Lodge; the St. John's Grand Lodge, as has already been shown, performed the functions of a Grand Lodge at
various times during the existence of the Massachusetts Grand Lodge
and up to the time of the union in 1792. The Massachusetts Grand
Lodge recognized St. John's as a legal Grand Body by the several acts
preparatory to the union and at the time of the union. Thus we see
there were two Grand Lodges in Massachusetts exercising concurrent
jurisdiction at the time that England granted to Prince Hall and his
associates a charter for African Lodge, No. 459. If two Grand Lodges
could, as they did, exercise concurrent jurisdiction, why not three?
Secondly, the Massachusetts Grand Lodge did not exercise jurisdiction
over all the Lodges of its claimed constituency, for, as we have already
shown, St. Peter's and Tyrian did not give their allegiance thereto until a considerable time after its organization—Tyrian, in September,
1794, and St. Peter's, in March, 1795; St. Andrew's Lodge absolutely refused to recognize the Massachusetts Grand Lodge as a Grand
Lodge and did not even come under the jurisdiction of the United
Grand Lodge until 1810, up to which time it worked under the authority of the Grand Lodge of Scotland and paid dues to that body,
severing its connection therefrom, not by revolution, but by regular
withdrawal and with the consent of the Grand Lodge of Scotland.

Again, we see that instead of one Grand Lodge exercising exclusive territorial jurisdiction, there are four exercising concurrent
jurisdiction, viz., the St. John's Grand Lodge, the Massachusetts
Grand Lodge, the Grand Lodge of England, and the Grand Lodge of
Scotland. Which is it, exclusive or concurrent territorial jurisdiction?

If the establishment of African Lodge, No. 459, was a violation of the rights of Massachusetts Grand Lodge, then why was not the existence of St. John's Grand Lodge a violation? Why was not the continued existence of St. Andrew's Lodge until 1810 a violation? If the manifesto of December 6th, 1782, is the basis upon which the Massachusetts Grand Lodge asserts claim to exclusive jurisdiction, and declares the existence of African Lodge a violation of its rights, why not make the same declaration concerning St. Andrew's Lodge? If the union of the two Grand Lodges in 1792 gave to the new Grand Lodge exclusive jurisdiction, and made all Lodges not allying themselves thereto illegal and clandestine, why should African Lodge, No. 459, be so denominated and St. Andrew's Lodge excepted? African Lodge, No. 459, was known to be in active existence in 1792, for it is of record that some of the white Masons of Boston were received as visitors therein; was she invited to become a part of the new organization in 1792? There is no record to show it. It is of record, though, that St. Andrew's Lodge was invited and that it refused to join with them, yet St. Andrew's, after defying the authority of the Massachusetts Grand Lodge for nearly thirty-three years is welcomed into its fold as a just and legal and regular Lodge, while African Lodge is denounced as clandestine, irregular, and illegal. On the one hand is the St. Andrew's Lodge, organized in 1752, with nine clandestine made Masons, standing out alone in open defiance to all the manifestos and articles of constitution of the Grand Lodge of Massachusetts, and yet received and welcomed with much joy; on the other hand stands African Lodge, No. 459, with as pure a parentage and as legal an organization as ever Mason had, willing to come under the authority of the Grand Lodge of Massachusetts, yet denied and villified. Need I ask why was this? And yet, all through this land the cry goes up concerning the violation of the territory of Massachusetts Grand Lodge by the organization of African Lodge, No. 459, but not a word against the acts of St. Andrew's Lodge, under the Grand Lodge of Scotland, from 1777 to 1810. The words of Bro. Joseph Robbins, of Illinois, so fittingly express our feelings on this point that we quote them:

" Isolated, ridiculed, denied the sympathy and support to which, as members of a universal brotherhood, they felt themselves entitled, and smarting under a sense of bitter wrong, is it strange that they yielded to that desire for human fellowship to which all races of men are subject, and sought to create means for its gratification [referring to the organization of Lodges at Philadelphia and Providence]? They would have been something more or less than human had they done otherwise. Whether an equal number of white Masons, with the same or less claim to recognition, would not long ago have been gathered into itself, is a question that may well be taken home by the Grand Lodge which, in the beautiful language of Bro. Gardner, 'stands upon the high vantage ground of this Catholic society, and recognizes the great principles which must underlie an institution which has a home on the continents and on the islands of the sea.'"

We now come to the general question of "Exclusive Territorial Jurisdiction." It is claimed that our Grand Lodges by occupying territory in common with the white Grand Lodges of this country violate this doctrine, and are therefore illegal. Our idea of illegality, as applied to Masonic bodies, means a violation of some Masonic principle universal in its application and fundamental in its character. Is this true of the doctrine of exclusive territorial jurisdiction. We think not. It is American in its origin; is not recognized outside of the United States, and was not known or thought of until enacted by the Grand Lodge of Massachusetts in the latter part of the last century. The history of its origin is thus recorded by Bro. Gardner in his address to the Grand Lodge of Massachusetts in 1870:

"The institution of Freemasonry, which numbered among its firmest adherents such revolutionists as Webb, Revere, Morton, and a host of others who followed in the footsteps of Warren, could not long withstand the influence of freedom, and Massachusetts set the example of a *revolution in Masonic government* [italics ours] which has been followed successfully by every State in the Union. It has become the American system, or, as the committee of New Hampshire call it, 'The American Doctrine of Grand Lodge Jurisdiction.'"

Here we have a dogma enunciated in the form of a simple resolution, the product of a REVOLUTION *in Masonic government*, which, at the behest of a single Grand Lodge, the entire Masonic world must accept as a fundamental Masonic principle. This is indeed an assumption of authority that might well cause us to ask, Whither are we drifting? We look in vain for its fundamental quality; and its universality is limited to a single nation who find in it a safe cloak under which to hide their prejudices against the negro Mason.

We quote further from Brother Gardner on this matter:

"The 'American doctrine of Grand Lodge jurisdiction' briefly stated is this: Three regularly chartered Lodges existing in any State or Territory have the right to establish a Grand Lodge therein. Such Grand Lodge, when lawfully organized, has sole, absolute, and exclusive jurisdiction over the three degrees of craft Masonry, over the Lodges and their members, and over all Masons, unaffiliated as well as affiliated, in such State or Territory.   No other Grand Lodge whatever can lawfully interfere with this jurisdiction, and can neither establish Lodges in such State, nor continue any authority over bodies which it might properly have exercised prior to the organization of such Lodge therein.

"By the erection of a Grand Lodge in such State, all Masonic power over what is popularly called Blue Masonry are merged in it, and henceforth it exists therein supreme and sovereign over a jurisdiction which it can never divide nor share with any other Masonic Grand body in the world.

"The several States of the United States of America, the Territories when legally organized as such by Congress, and the District of Columbia, are each recognized as separate and independent jurisdictions in which Grand Lodges may be established.

"This is the American doctrine most religiously and Masonically adhered to by the craftsmen of the United States, and which our brethren upon the other side of the Atlantic *must* accede to, recognize, and support."

We have given all of Brother Gardner's "doctrine" in order that our readers may see what a master of rhetoric he is, and how with legal exactness he covers every possible point.   We call this Brother Gardner's "doctrine," for we believe it to have been evolved from his mind in the seclusion of his study while burning the midnight oil; or, perhaps, it may be one of the "local regulations" of Massachusetts. We are certain it is not a "general regulation," for we have searched Masonic records o'er and o'er to find the time when, and the place where, the General Assembly met to adopt this measure.   And still more are we certain that it is not a "landmark," for it bears neither the mark of universality or antiquity; therefore, we assert it as our belief, that it is Brother Gardner's doctrine.

That it is not universal, is proven by language used, wherein it is stated that "our brethren on the other side of the Atlantic *must* accede to, recognize, and support it."   I think our brethren on this side of the Atlantic will have quite a task on hand when they attempt to force universal obedience to this "doctrine."   We can not take more time in the analysis of this wonderful document than to say that historical evidence is at hand to refute every clause of which it is constructed.

With reference to the first clause, neither of the Grand Lodges of New Hampshire or Massachusetts was formed in accordance therewith, although there were more than three regularly chartered Lodges in each State.

With reference to the second clause, instances are numerous where other Grand Lodges than the ones formed in accordance with this doctrine, have exercised jurisdiction over the three degrees of Craft Masonry; for instance, the Grand Lodge of Scotland in the case of Massachusetts, and also in Quebec; the Grand Lodge of England in Massachusetts, and also in Canada, and in New South Wales; the Grand Lodge of Virginia in West Virginia; the Grand Lodge of Hamburg in New York; the Grand Lodge of Missouri in New Mexico; the two Grand Lodges in South Carolina; the three Grand Lodges in New York; the two Grand Lodges in Louisiana; the two Grand Lodges of England; the three Grand Lodges of Prussia, and numerous other examples that might be cited to show the correctness of our position and the absurdity of the "American doctrine of exclusive territorial jurisdiction." Massachusetts herself, in the preamble to the resolutions adopted in 1782, admits the existence of concurrent jurisdiction in these words:

"That in the history of our craft we find that in England there are two Grand Lodges independent of each, in Scotland the same, and in Ireland their Grand Lodge and Grand Master are independent of either."

As these criticisms apply to the first two clauses, so they also apply to the remaining clauses.

The true theory of Grand Lodge jurisdiction is correctly set forth in Article III of the series of articles engrafted into the constitution of the Massachusetts Grand Lodge, in 1782, as follows:

"That the power and authority of the said Grand Lodge be construed to extend throughout the Commonwealth of Massachusetts, and to any of the United States, where none other is erected, over such Lodges *only* as this Grand Lodge has constituted, or shall constitute."

This, we have said, is the true theory of Grand Lodge jurisdiction. Every Grand Lodge has authority and jurisdiction over all the Lodges of its own creation and none others, no matter where they may be situated. And in the organization of a Grand Lodge in a territory where there are Lodges subordinate to different Grand Lodges, the new Grand Lodge acquires jurisdiction over the Lodges only that constitute it. The right does not reside in any body of Masons to force the Lodges outside of the new Grand Lodge to surrender their old warrants and take out new ones under the new Grand Lodge. A warranted Lodge has rights that can not be abrogated by a simple resolution; one of these rights is to retain its membership in the Grand Lodge of which it forms a constituent part; it can not be forced out of its mother

Grand Lodge. To do so would be a violation of every principle un-derlying our institution.

We repeat, again, that the doctrine of exclusive territorial jurisdic-tion is an American dogma, unmasonic in character and not supported by any law or principle known to Masonry; before the institution of Grand Lodges the Masonic jurisdiction of a Lodge was universal and concurrent with that of all others; and since, it has been the same, excepting in America, where a false system has been foisted onto the craft. It had its origin in revolution and aims to be kept alive by force and assumption.

As a proof of this it is only necessary to review the proceedings of the various Grand Lodges of America to find resolution after resolu-tion being adopted to bolster up this false doctrine.

And yet, after all the legislation in reference thereto, we find the American Grand Lodges not adhering to it; for the records show that numbers of Grand Lodges, while holding concurrent jurisdiction with other Grand Lodges, have been received and acknowledged as Sover-eign Grand Lodges. This is true in the case of the Grand Lodge of Quebec, the Grand Lodge of New South Wales, the Grand Lodge of ● West Virginia, the Grand Lodge of Dakota, the Grand Lodge of New Mexico, and others that could be named.

Although this is called the "American Doctrine," yet there are numbers of American Masons who can not shut their eyes to the fact that it violates the relation that must always exist between a subordi-nate Lodge and its mother Grand Lodge, and therefore their sound sense and judgment will not permit them to subscribe to it. To prove this, we quote the expressions of learned American Masonic jurists in relation to the same :

Brother Bell, of New Hampshire, said, in 1869 :

"The American doctrine of Grand Lodge jurisdiction has grown up since then [meaning the establishment of African Lodge], and is not elsewhere fully received *now*."

Bro. John D. Vincil, of Missouri, in reviewing the Proceedings of the Grand Lodge of New Mexico, in 1880, says:

"The questions between our Grand Lodge and New Mexico re-main unsettled. The Grand Lodge of New Mexico has proclaimed that the charter of Silver City Lodge, No. 465, is under arrest. That Lodge was chartered by the Grand Lodge of Missouri, October 17, 1873, before the Grand Lodge of New Mexico was formed. As the *life* of Silver City Lodge was derived from the Grand Lodge of Missouri, so its *allegiance* must be rendered to this Grand Lodge. By no act has Silver City Lodge forfeited the *life* given it by the Missouri Grand Lodge. Its allegiance to the creating power—Missouri—must continue until transferred to another by its own act, or its mother Grand Lodge."

Brother Vincil enunciates true Masonic doctrine in the above. We now quote from the Proceedings of Minnesota, 1880, in relation to the dispute between the Grand Lodges of Minnesota and Dakota:

"*Resolved*, That any Masonic body holding authority from this Grand Lodge within Dakota Territory, so long as it shall desire to continue its connection with this, its paternal Grand Lodge, be permitted to do so, and that this M. W. Grand Lodge will defend and maintain its rights, and exercise authority over it, until such time as by its own free will and accord it shall desire to sever connection with us."

This seems to be decided opposition to "exclusive territorial jurisdiction."

The Grand Secretary of Dakota, Bro. A. T. C. Pierson, says, upon the "dogma of exclusive jurisdiction:"

"The doctrine is declared to be 'an outgrowth of the declaration of the independence of the colonies from the mother country.' 'Although an *innovation on the practices of the Grand Lodges then in existence*,' it has since become popular and has very generally [not entirely so] obtained among the American Grand Lodges. European Grand Lodges *have never recognized* the doctrine."

Bro. A. S. Wait, of New Hampshire, in 1881, in reviewing Illinois, utters the following sound doctrine in relation to exclusive jurisdiction :

"We have long been of the opinion that the relations of the various Grand Lodges was a system of *Masonic comity*, and not of positive law."

After discoursing further upon this subject to show the absurdity of the "doctrine," he says:

"We may as well go farther and say, what we think, that upon the regular formation of a Grand Lodge, all Lodges within the territory of its rightful jurisdiction ought to give in their adhesion to it, and the Grand Lodges from which they received their charters ought, from motives of fraternal comity to advise such a course. But we neither think that Lodges declining to join in the organization of the new Grand body become extinct by its formation, nor that by refusing to give in adhesion to it they become illegitimate or clandestine. The whole matter is one of comity, in which no Grand Lodge can coerce another. And if any 'American doctrine' has obtained to the contrary of this, it ought speedily to be repudiated by American Masons, as well as by the fraternity elsewhere."

From· the Proceedings of the Grand Lodge of Nova Scotia, 1880, we cull the following from the Grand Master's address as bearing upon this topic :   •

"Royal Standard Lodge, holding under the Grand Lodge of England, is with us a pattern Lodge in matters of ritual and discipline ; working side by side with us, a healthy emulation is produced, and both parties are the better for it. By invitation I lately visited this. Lodge, accompanied by the Grand Officers and a large body of Nova. Scotia Masons, and the cordial feelings reciprocally expressed gave the strongest proof that the existence of an English Lodge in our midst was working no injury to the craft here."

Here we have another evidence of the unsoundness of all objections. to concurrent jurisdiction.

Many more quotations could be given showing that there are many Masons in America that do not subscribe to the " American Doctrine ;" we have one other, however, which is so full and complete that we close our quotations with it. We take it from Bro. Wait's report to the Grand Lodge of New Hampshire in 1881. He says :

" But one subject which has been growing in prominence for some years has, during that under review, assumed an importance which seems to render all others of comparatively slight moment. It is what is known in this country (what its name is elsewhere we are not informed) as 'The American Doctrine' of Grand Lodge jurisdiction.

"What precisely this doctrine is, which has been for a few years past invoked by that name, has not, so far as we are aware, ever been precisely defined; and, what is quite certain, there is no existing power capable either of defining it authoritatively in theory, or prescribing its practical limits."

After giving its probable origin in the resolutions of 1782 and 1797, and giving Gardner's amplifications on the same, he says :

" It is not claimed for this doctrine, so far as we have heard, that it is a law of Masonry, belonging to its fundamental or essential principles, or that it obtains elsewhere than on the American continent ; and it is quite certain that the doctrine, with these amplifications, is. repudiated among Grand Lodges and Masons of the old world.

" If we are to judge of this doctrine, thus interpreted, by its fruits, we have little hesitation in saying that it possesses small title to general favor. It has, so far as we have observed, proved a Pandora's. box, out of which have sprung nothing but discord and confusion. We have as its outgrowth those unseemly contentions which at the present time disfigure our Institution in this country, and can scarcely fail to make it a by-word and a laughing-stock among the brethren elsewhere, while producing actual estrangement between the Masons of this country and Europe.

"We believe that, when our brethren of America shall have seen enough of edicts of non-intercourse and non-recognition; when they shall have seen enough of discord and confusion; when, instead of Grand Lodge supremacy as the end of Masonry, their hearts shall yearn for the universal manifestation of the principles of brotherly love, which ought to unite the whole human species in one family, and conciliates true friendship among the race universal, they will be ready to eschew a doctrine which will prove as surely in the future, as it has in the past, potent for evil while powerless for good."

Further presentation of facts and opinions is unnecessary, for we believe sufficient have been adduced to show that the granting of a warrant to African Lodge, No. 459, by the Grand Lodge of England, in 1784, was no violation of the jurisdictional rights of the Massachusetts Grand Lodge, either real or assumed; and, furthermore, that the occupancy of any State, or Territory, by two or more Grand or Subordinate Lodges is no violation of any fundamental Masonic law or principle. Therefore, we conclude that the claim that our Grand Lodges are illegal because they occupy the same territory as white Grand Lodges, is not well founded.

There may be many who will not agree at present with our conclusions concerning this matter, but we believe the time will come when this "American Doctrine" will be abandoned, and, in its stead, the true Masonic idea of concurrent jurisdiction, based upon genuine authority, will be the universally accepted doctrine.

We have now met and answered all the reasons that are given for our non-recognition. We feel that we have clearly proven that the reasons for our objection do not rest upon Masonic law, and have neither historical fact nor reasonable presumption for a basis. We feel that with fair-minded men—men desiring to be just—there can no longer be any doubt that Prince Hall and his Associates were made Masons in a legal Lodge; that they were so recognized as such by the Grand Lodge of England; that the Grand Lodge of England granted them a warrant to exist as a Lodge; that the warrant was received in this country by Prince Hall and his associates, and that they were legally organized under it; that the warrant so received was a true and authentic document; that it was never returned to England for correction, but remained in this country in the hands of its proper custodians, in its original form, void of all mutilations; that the granting of the warrant was no violation of the territorial rights of the Massachusetts Grand Lodge; that there is strong presumptive evidence that Prince Hall was deputized as a Provincial Grand Master; that there were fair and reasonable grounds upon which Prince Hall could base his action in exercising the powers of a Provincial Grand Master; that the African Grand Lodge, formed in Boston in 1808, was as regular as other Grand Lodges formed by white Masons prior and subsequent thereto; that in the death of Prince Hall, in 1807, the rights of succession were no more lost than when Warren died on Bunker Hill; that the removing of African Lodge from the lists of the Grand Lodge of England, in 1813, had no more disastrous effect upon said Lodge than upon the many white American Lodges that were removed at the same and prior times; that the declaration of independence, made by the African Lodge in 1827, destroyed no more of its rights than those of the white Lodges which had made similar declarations at different times; that the organization of a National Grand Lodge, in 1847, destroyed none of the legal rights of the Subordinate and Grand Lodges entering therein; that we are not free-born is an objection based upon a false idea, and in opposition to that tenet which the "brotherhood of man because of the Fatherhood of God"; and that the "Doctrine of Exclusive Territorial Jurisdiction" is but a form of government, local in its application, having no foundation in Masonic principle, or even General Regulations, and, therefore, having no binding force upon the government of the Fraternity.

While we feel that we have clearly proven the justness of our claims to recognition as legal and regular Masons; while we know there are large numbers of white Masons who acknowledge the justness of these claims, and stand ready and willing to try us and not deny us, we, also, feel and know that there is a vaster and a mightier number who, knowing all these things to be true, yet reject us and deny us. You ask what motive can impel these men—men whose eloquent utterances, in chaste and beautiful language, have bid the world to pause and gaze upon the matchless symmetry of our grand and noble institution, and contemplate in awe the grandeur and sublimity of its principles—to reject the truth? It is that slimy-coated and cold-blooded serpent of prejudice against the negro. You see it in every walk of life, in the workshop and in the counting-house; in the feeble and tottering imbecile and in the little, prattling child; where e'er you turn, the monster, with his ever-open, glassy eye, is staring at you. No place is secure from his intrusion; go to the halls of justice and you will find him there; and even within the sacred portals of God's tabernacles does he stealthily crawl, not even sparing the altar where the humble Christian kneels to take the consecrated emblems of our Lord and

Saviour. This is why we are denied; this is why we are rejected; this is why we are termed clandestine, illegal, and irregular. Do we speak at random? Are we giving play to the fancy? Would that we were, for then our fair institution would not have its escutcheon tarnished with falsehood and hypocrisy. But the recorded expressions of our traducers are before us, and we can not say nay when it is yea. That you may know we but speak the truth, we lay before you the utterances and acts of both individuals and organizations in reference to the negro Mason.

In a letter written to Bro. John D. Caldwell, Grand Secretary of the Grand Lodge of Ohio (white), by Ill.·. Bro. Albert Pike, Sov.·. Grand Commander of the Supreme Council, A. A. S. R., Southern Jurisdiction, bearing date of September 13, 1875, he says:

"Our people only *stave off* the question by saying that negro Masons here are clandestine. Prince Hall Lodge was as regular a Lodge as any Lodge created by competent authority. . . . .

"I think there is no middle ground between rigid exclusion of negroes or recognition and affiliation with the whole mass.

"I am not inclined to meddle in the matter. I took my obligations to white men, not to negroes. When I have to accept negroes as *brothers* or leave Masonry, I shall leave it.

"I am interested to keep the Ancient and Accepted Rite uncontaminated, in *our* country at least, by the leprosy of negro association."

We have from Brother (?) Pike, first, that we are as regular as any other class of Masons, and immediately thereafter, that between recognizing them as brothers or leaving Masonry, he will leave Masonry. Is this prejudice or not? And yet this same Mason (?) stands up in the presence of a great multitude in 1868 in St. Louis, and says:

"God pity the man who will not lay on the altar of Masonry every feeling of ambition, every feeling of ill-will in his heart toward a brother Mason. Freemasonry is one faith, one great religion, one great common altar, around which all men, of all tongues and all languages, can assemble. And Masonry will never be true to her mission till we all join hands, heart to heart and hand to hand, around the altar of Masonry, with a determination that Masonry shall become at some time worthy of her pretensions—no longer a pretender to that which is good; but that she shall be an apostle of *peace, good-will, charity,* and *toleration.*"

What think you of a man professing to be a Mason uttering such sentiments as these and then declaring that he would leave Masonry before recognizing a negro as a brother?

God pity Brother Pike and the thousands of canting hypocrites like him.

In 1870, the Chairman of the Committee on Foreign Correspondence, of Virginia, says:

"Respecting negro Masons, it behooves us to speak with unabated breath. In the palmiest days of royal despotism the hand of Douglass was his own, and never will Southern Masons acquiesce in the overthrow of ancient landmarks, subjecting them to the necessity of meeting upon the level with their former slaves."

Brother Lewis, of New York, says, in reviewing Alabama:

"Brother Penic seems to apprehend trouble from the negro business in the future. We do not see that there is any need of apprehension. It is not within the bounds of probability that any regular Grand Lodge will consent to swell its jurisdiction by the creation of negro Lodges; but if the taste of any should run in that direction, the rest of us still retain the right to withhold our recognition of that kind of work, and to close the doors of our Lodges against any and all likely to disturb our peace and harmony."

Here is certainly sufficient evidence of a very bitter prejudice against the negro, and these examples might be multiplied by the score, but we do not deem it necessary; neither shall we review the action of the various Grand Lodges, excepting New Jersey, in which this question of the recognition of negro Masons has been introduced, more than to say that in many of them may be found resolution after resolution setting forth the inferiority of the negro and his unfitness to become a Mason, or to be recognized as one if already made. The history of Alpha Lodge, No. 16, of New Jersey, is familiar to all Masonic students, but for the uninformed we quote from the record. The Lodge was regularly organized and duly warranted, after which it made a number of colored men Masons; this raised considerable excitement, not only in New Jersey, but throughout the United States, so much so that the warrant was arrested; the Lodge was finally allowed to die, and the colored brethren made therein set adrift without chart or compass. Now, these brethren having been made in a legal and regular Lodge under the authority of the Grand Lodge of New Jersey, which held fraternal relations with all the other Grand Lodges in America, were certainly not clandestine; then why all this excitement and subsequent arrest of warrant? Simply because they were negroes, and the curse of prejudice was against them. And this curse has followed us here in America, wherever and whenever we have presented our claims for recognition. If we have applied as profanes we have been met with either the silent, but sure and certain black ball, or with the mandatory resolution of a Grand Lodge hurled against us with all the force of a unanimous ballot; if, as an organization, with humble manner apologizing for our existence, and with agreement to surrender our legal rights, meaningless resolutions embodying conclusions that are as false as they are unjust are given to us; if we come in the upright stature of men and Masons demanding what is our right, we are met with parliamentary quibbles. The experience of history teaches us that the animus of all these varied actions has its seat in the prejudice of the white American against the negro.

This is the history of the past; what the future may bring forth we know not, yet we do not despair of ultimate success in having all our rights as Masons accorded to us. With the steady acquirement of civil and political rights, and all other rights pertaining to humanity, must come a recognition of our Masonic rights. It has already commenced in foreign lands, where, in France, and Italy, and Germany, and Hungary, and Peru, and Dominica, our representatives, received and accredited as such, are proclaiming to the world the true Masonic doctrine of a universal brotherhood.

And may we not say that it is dawning in America? Has there not been some progress, some advancement made toward the right? We think so. In 1847, the Grand Lodge of Ohio (white), under the impulse of prejudice against the negro, "*Resolved*, that in the opinion of this Grand Lodge it would be inexpedient, and tend to ruin the present harmony of the fraternity to admit persons of color, so called, into the fraternity of Free and Accepted Masons within the jurisdiction of this Grand Lodge."

In 1875, the progessive spirit of justice and right had made sufficient advancement for the brotherhood to see that a "New Day" was dawning, and that a "New Duty" was incumbent upon them. And to Bro. John D. Caldwell, Grand Secretary of the Grand Lodge of Ohio (white), must the credit be given for awakening the craft to a sense of the responsibilities which they assume in failing to perform this duty.

And in the same year, under the influence of this same progressive spirit, the temper of the Grand Lodge that adopted the above resolution had become sufficiently modified to permit the reception and reference to a committee of the following eloquent letter, written by Bro. F. I. Werner, W. M. of Hanselman Lodge, No. 208, Cincinnati,

Ohio, every line of which proves him a Mason in the truest and fullest meaning of the word:

"CINCINNATI, in October, 1875.

"*To the Grand Lodge of Masons for the State of Ohio:*

"BRETHREN:—I beg leave to respectfully present for your kind consideration the following memorial:

"The United Grand Lodge of Masons of Germany have, at their convention in Darmstadt, in the month of May, 1875, passed the following resolution in relation to the colored Grand Lodges of America.

'With regard to the motions made by the Grand Lodge, 'Prince Hall,' and the Grand Lodge of Ohio (colored), the convention of Grand Lodges declares that these Grand Lodges appear properly constituted, and that the German Lodges will accord to the members of those Lodges and of their sister Lodges, without reserve and joyfully, acceptance into their Lodges.'

"Upon reading this resolution, the following questions presented themselves to my mind: What influence will this action have upon the discussions of our own Grand Lodge? Will they, at last, compelled by outward pressure, take up the subject of Negro Lodges in earnest, or will silence and inaction be repeatedly the watchword, as it has been time and again, allowing prejudice against the race and color to override those very principles of justice and brotherly love we like to glory in so much? Or will the whole discussion, if taken up at all, terminate in a fruitless and passionate debate over a transgression upon our respective jurisdictions? Very likely the latter, I thought.

"And now, brethren, in my humble opinion, common humanity, self-respect, and the highest interests of our beloved brotherhood imperiously demand from us to at least ascertain the facts respecting colored Lodges. The men constituting the same either are Masons or are not. If they are, we have no earthly right, and no excuse whatever, to let things go on as heretofore, and not to recognize them as such. If they are *not* Masons, if they are impostors, then we must proclaim it to the world. Justice to ourselves demands it.

"It would be contrary to Masonic principles and to Masonic philosophy not to recognize them, if they are Masons—all prejudices of white people against negroes notwithstanding. It would, on the other hand, be the grossest neglect of our duty as Masons not to unvail to the world's vision their imposition, if they are *not* Masons. It would be, finally, on our part, as men and Masons, an exhibition of extreme weakness and (I hope I do not offend you) cowardice, if we did not, at the earliest moment, put an end to this anomalous state of affairs in the Masonic world by a speedy examination into the same, and manly, decisive action thereafter.

"Are we afraid of the light shed on the subject by such examination? If we are, let us abandon our proud proclamation, 'Let there be light!' If we are not, let us have speedy action, and rid the Masonic world of an unqualified misery, which makes us feel uneasy as often as we venture to discuss it, and creates serious doubts in our own minds as often as we declare the supremacy of Masonic principles.

"In view of this, and in consideration that this negro question should be looked squarely into the face, as it will create not less an 'irrepressible conflict' in the Masonic world than it did in the political world, and in further consideration that we, as true Masons, are ever ready to seek after truth and deal with justice I present the following for your action

"Believing that the Grand Lodge of Masons for the State of Ohio is aware of the existence in this State of organized bodies of colored citizens, who claim to be in possession of the *signs* and *secrets* of Free and Accepted Ancient Freemasonry, the undersigned regards it as the paramount duty of the Grand Lodge of *white Masons* to appoint a committee, whose duty it shall be to inquire into the legitimacy of said claim ; and if, upon examination, it shall appear well founded, then I respectfully urge that the necessary steps be taken to *utilize* this *timber*, rather than condemn it as *rotten* and *unfit* for use, without having subjected it to a *fair, candid, and impartial test.*

"Very respectfully, F. I. WERNER, W. M.,
"*Hanselmann Lodge, No.* 208, *F. and A. M.*"

Would that every Mason throughout our land had implanted within him the seeds of such noble thoughts as are given expression to in this letter; then might Masonry indeed be true to her profession.

In this same year, from the Grand East of the Grand Lodge of Ohio (white), Bro. Asa H. Battin, in the spirit of true Masonry, utters these words:

"In this great centennial year, whilst liberty and equality are shed abroad through our great nation, is it not right and proper that we, as Masons, shall at least attempt to bring about, by proper means and in a legal manner, a union of these two Grand Lodges in one State? If there is any illegality in the organization of either, let it be healed. It has been done before, and it can be again. Let us, then, with that charity and liberality which characterizes all Masons, extend the fraternal hand of fellowship to our brethren of every nation, clime, race, and kindred under heaven. And let it be, too, not only in name, but in spirit and in truth. Let us illustrate our teachings by example. And as the crowning glory of republican government is the equality of all men before the law, so should the crowning glory of our Mystic Temple be the equality of all men without regard to race or previous condition. Brethren, this question must be met. We may, for the present, pass by on the other side; we may look upon it, fold our mantles around us, and pass on; but the Good Samaritan is coming, has come, and is pouring the oil of fellowship into the wounds, binding up the bruises and taking the sufferers to his own house. Why should we longer delay? I am vain enough to believe that we are capable of meeting it fairly. I have faith in our people. I have faith in their sense of justice and magnanimity. I can not believe that many years can elapse before the great body of Colored Masons will be recognized as a part of the great Masonic family, and accorded their rights as such. I have candidly expressed my opinion, and I leave the matter to you for your consideration, earnestly hoping that you may have wisdom to devise some means by which the Masons of Ohio may be united into one family and brotherly love prevail. If within the great centennial year this result can be accomplished, or measures taken looking to such result, we shall have reason to rejoice that the march of progress is onward and upward, and the universal brotherhood of man, on the Western Continent, fully, fairly, and unchangeably established, and the world made better by our example.''

Brother Werner's letter and Brother Battin's remarks were referred to a special committee, who, in the same spirit as the writers thereof, and in the defense of truth and justice, certifying to our legal existence and paving the way to a just adjudication of our claims, unanimously submitted the following report:

''PROPOSED RECOGNITION OF THE COLORED GRAND LODGE OF OHIO.

''Your committee to whom was referred so much of the annual address of the Most Worshipful Grand Master, and accompanying documents, as relates to the so-called colored Lodges, and more especially the colored Grand Lodge of Free and Accepted Masons of the State of Ohio, have given the subject careful consideration, and respectfully submit the following:

''We do not propose, nor do we deem it necessary at this time, to enter into the history of the origin of so-called colored Freemasonry in this country. That subject has been fully discussed in nearly all the Grand Lodges and Masonic periodicals of this country for more than twenty-five years past.

''Your Committee deem it sufficient to say that *they* are satisfied *beyond all question* that colored Freemasonry had a legitimate beginning in this country, as much so as any other Freemasonry; in fact, it came from *the same source.*

''Your Committee will not attempt, at this time, to investigate as to the transmission of this legitimate beginning down to the present time, when we find more than forty Subordinate Lodges and a Grand Lodge of so-called colored Freemasons, and an aggregate of more than eight hundred members in the State of Ohio. Your Committee have only to say that such is the fact.

''Your Committee have the most satisfactory and conclusive evidence that these colored Freemasons practice the very same rites and ceremonies, and have substantially the same esoteric or secret modes of recognition as are practiced by ourselves and by the universal family of Freemasons throughout the world.

'' The question of the recognition of these colored Freemasons has long been before this Grand Body, and your Committee feel that its importance is pressing upon us, and demanding prompt, serious, and decided action.

"Your Committee, therefore, offer for adoption the following resolution:

"*Resolved*, by the 'Grand Lodge of the Most Ancient and Honorable Fraternity of Free and Accepted Masons of the State of Ohio,' that this Grand body will recognize the so-called Grand Lodge of colored Freemasons of the State of Ohio as a legitimate and independent Grand Lodge, on condition that the so-called colored Grand Lodge shall change its constitutional title, so that it shall read as follows: '*The African Grand Lodge of Free and Accepted Masons of the State of Ohio.*' And if the said so-called colored Grand Lodge shall accept this recognition and make the suggested change in its constitutional title, then, and in that case, upon said action being reported to the M. W. Grand Master of this Grand Lodge, under the seal of said body, then the M. W. Grand Master is hereby authorized and instructed to issue his proclamation to the subordinates to this Grand Lodge and to the Grand Lodges throughout the world, with which we are in fraternal correspondence, recognizing the said so-called colored Grand Lodge as an Independent Grand Lodge in the State of Ohio, under the title of '*The African Grand Lodge of Free and Accepted Masons of the State of Ohio.*'

"Respectfully submitted, L. V. BIERCE, C. A. WOODWARD, E. T. CARSON, L. H. PIKE." F. WILLMER,

These papers will form an important part of the Masonic literature of Ohio, and they will illuminate the pages of Masonic history with a brilliancy of such power that the names thereon will be seen of generations yet unborn.

But what of the "report of the committee?" Did the Grand Lodge adopt it? Alas, it did not! A "point of order," a parliamentary quibble, which the Grand Master, Bro. Chas. A. Woodward, ruled as not well taken, decided its fate. From the Grand Master's decision an appeal was taken, which resulted in three hundred and thirty-two votes being cast to "sustain the decision of the Grand Master as the opinion of the Grand Lodge," and three hundred and ninety votes against the same, a majority of only fifty-eight against the Grand Master, out of a total of seven hundred and twenty-two votes. If only thirty other brethren had voted " aye," what a change there would have been in the Masonic history of Ohio. No need, there would be now, to write these lines. Ohio would indeed have become *an apostle of peace, good-will, charity, and toleration.*' But no, it was not to be so; the wily Cunningham, like he at Thermopylae, who betrayed the noble Spartan band by showing to the enemy the secret pass, led the opponents of truth and justice to victory by a trick of shrewd parliamentary practice.   Although error and injustice triumphed for the time being, the influence of these three hundred and thirty-two advocates of right —these three hundred and thirty-two exponents of the progress of the true spirit of Masonry—will be felt, and Ohio, moving forward under the inspiration of this influence, must, per force of its power, "once more unto the breach," and raise her standard for "equality and fraternity."

Masons of Ohio, Masons of America, Masons of the world, wheresoever dispersed, the negro Mason of America stands before you today as a just and upright Mason, and as such demands that you shall try him by the square of virtue, and having tried him and found him just and true, he further demands that you deny him not, but that you receive him and accept him, and accord unto him all of right that may belong to him.   He does not make this demand because he is a negro, neither does he ask that you do this as a favor; but he demands it because he is a Mason as you are, and because his right to the title of Free and Accepted Mason is equal to yours—no more, no less.

Do not be frightened and think that we ask this act of justice on your part for the purpose of gratifying an idle curiosity to peer into your Lodge rooms, or to force ourselves into your company against your desire; we do it for nothing of the sort.   We know, from experience, that the curiosity will be on your side, and, thanks for our close adherence to the rites of our profession, we feel amply able to satisfy it; we know that *our* Lodge rooms will be the ones most frequently visited, and we assure you that you will always receive the fraternal welcome of a true Mason.

But this is why we demand it: We have always been taught that Masonry is universal in its character; that neither race nor creed can debar one from an entrance therein; that the beggar and the prince are alike equals within its closely tiled doors, and that its "central idea is the 'brotherhood of man because of the Fatherhood of God.'" Because of all these things; because we desire that the stigma of hypocrisy, deceit, and injustice shall be forever blotted out; because we desire that our ancient and noble and grand institution shall have a name honored of all men and all nations, in all countries and in all climes, of all creeds and all faiths; and because we desire that our institution shall be as beauteous and glorious as the noonday sun at meridian height, darting its rays to the North and the South, to the East and the West, bathing all humanity in a glorious flood of the sunshine

of peace and good-will, is why we demand that you bury your prejudices and prove yourselves Masons indeed.

We have nothing to gain in your legal recognition of us as Masons;
the gain is all for you and the institution of Freemasonry. That we
are just and legal Masons is so well established that it is now beyond
the power of man to controvert it. For more than one hundred years
we have existed as Free and Accepted Masons; we have now commenced the second century of our existence as such; from the lowest
round of humility we have climbed far up the ladder of fame; from the
small beginning of fifteen black men, scoffed at, sneered at, insulted,
and ridiculed, we have grown to grand proportions, until to-day we command the respect of Masons in all parts of the world; what we are to-
day has been accomplished by our own exertions, isolated and rejected
as we have been; if, by our own exertions alone, we must build our
second century, we will make it more illustrious than the first; we will
proudly hold aloft our heads, and courageously fighting our battles,
we will neither give nor ask quarter.

Our task is done. If we have been tedious; if we have been ex-
cessive in the matter of quotations; if we have made repetitions, it
has only been to more forcibly impress you with the point presented,
and to sustain it with the strongest corroborative evidence.

In parting from you we again say, do what is just, not for our sake,
but for the sake of Masonry. You can not afford to do otherwise, for
the world is gazing upon you, and as you act, so will it judge.

If you shall continue to refuse to have the light of justice and
reason to illuminate your benighted intelligence, and shall refuse to
accord us those rights legally belonging to us, we will appeal to the
world at large for a judgment, and, as Free and Accepted Masons,
will go bravely forward in the cause of freedom and humanity, writing, in letters of blazing gold, the legend — Negro Masonry, the
essence of TRUTH, JUSTICE, BROTHERLY LOVE, EQUALITY and FRA-
TERNITY ! !

www.ingramcontent.com/pod-product-compliance
Lightning Source LLC
Chambersburg PA
CBHW051504270326
41933CB00021BA/3465